One Hundred Years of

Cocktail Designs and Designing Cocktails

DEDICATED TO
ALL OF THOSE WHO
HAVE HELPED EVALUATE
AND CRITIQUE THE
RECIPES CONTAINED
WITHIN THESE
PAGES OVER HUNDREDS OF
VERY LONG NIGHTS
AT THE BAR
AND MOST ESPECIALLY
THANKS TO
KELVIN WU
WITHOUT WHOM THIS
BOOK WOULD NOT
HAVE BEEN MADE POSSIBLE

TABLE OF CONTENTS

(continued on the next page)

FOREWORD

It has been over fifteen years now since I began writing my first book, *Cocktails of the South Pacific*. The first portion of that book was about my family's hundred years in the liquor industry along with some colorful history with Victor Bergeron ("Trader Vic"). I have not repeated any of that same history here. In the many years since that book was published, I have had the unusual opportunity to create cocktails for customers at my own bar with a virtually unlimited budget for experimentation. Every night and after hours, dozens of experiments were conducted, most of which were tasted and simply discarded—something almost no one could normally do. Two things emerged from all those years and literally tens of thousands of tests:

First, a sizeable collection of crafted recipes, but more important, a *system*. This is not like any other "cocktail book" because it is not merely a collection of recipes. This system explains how to minimize wasting ingredients with random experiments and to greatly increase the percentage of highly successful new cocktails you create. That is the focus of this book—showing you a tactical approach to mixology.

After understanding the ingredients themselves better in the first section, the scheme is revealed and then followed by many examples.

I was inspired to write this book because no other book contains this information, and possibly never will, considering the vast amount of resources and time that went into it. This is my best attempt to pass along what I have learned and discovered over a lifetime. I only hope it can help you, the reader, further your pursuit of excellence in mixology.

Greg Easter

≋ PLEASE READ THIS FIRST ≋

These are some important points to know before diving into recipes here.

WEIGHT NOT VOLUME

The quantities stated for every single recipe in this book were determined by weight, not volume. I use the electronic scale from Perfect Drink which accurately measures to 0.1 gram. Even if you do not have the Perfect Drink scale—which I highly recommend because it steps you through recipes using an app on your phone via bluetooth—get an accurate scale and measure by volume and not weight. Otherwise your measurements will be off throughout this book. Let me repeat that:

MANY MEASUREMENTS WILL BE WRONG IN THAT CASE!

The reason is density. Syrups weigh more than alcohol per unit volume. So if I wrote 15ml of a syrup, I mean 15 grams, which will be slightly less than 15ml if you want to be accurate. If you absolutely must measure by volume, shoot for a bit less for syrups and a bit more for overproof spirits. 151-proof rum is lighter than water, so 15 grams would be 1 to 2 ml less than the 15ml that might have been stated in the recipe. The easiest solution to this problem is to GET A SCALE and use it. This will be much faster and more accurate than the 18th century tools you have probably been using.

One word of caution about the Perfect Drink scale: The model sold through Amazon in the U.S. for about $95 is the correct one. In Europe there is a very cheap version made by a Chinese company that is not Bluetooth (it requires a cable and very few tablets and phones have that sort of connection these days). Get the real product, or just get any good scale that can read to 1/10 gram.

SOLVING AVAILABILITY ISSUES

Two of the most difficult problems in writing a cocktail recipe for other people to follow are:

1. The liquors available in one part of the world are often not available where the reader lives. This is especially extreme in

the difference between the United States and Europe. Plus, most nations in Europe have specialty alcoholic products that are only available by traveling to those nations and bringing them back in luggage. This would be a significant problem with recipes I created in Finland, because there are dozens of unusual products that almost no one reading this book will have regular access to. Recipes in this book do not call for those products. Substitutions have been made in some instances.

2. Individuals rarely have the budget of a large commercial bar, or the space to stock hundreds of different products (most of which will sit collecting dust).

These two complaints have been leveled against many high end cocktail books in recent years because bartenders seek to work with exotic spirits that consumers can't get, or can't afford to buy just for the sake of making a single drink. Those problems have largely been solved in this book. You can make most of these cocktails with ordinary ingredients using cordials that you can cook up in any kitchen inexpensively and without distillation. An appendix of the recipes for all of those is at the back.

The ingredients you make yourself are marked with an asterisk (*) next to them, so just look up their recipe in the index. These liqueurs and cordials will keep a long time when refrigerated, and even though they are a bit of a fiddle to make, a single batch is enough to last for many drinks. In one afternoon you can make almost all of them if you put your mind to it.

A few of those cordials and liqueurs are not used frequently in this book, but the recipe has been included to give you a sort of "chemistry set" to experiment with on your own. The flavors are all worthwhile and unlike anything you can buy.

YOU WILL NEED CITRUS OILS TO USE THIS BOOK

Lemon, Lime, Orange and Grapefruit. They are available online. Some say they are for aroma use, but don't worry because you are using a tiny fraction of a drop in most drinks. Simply go to Amazon and search for CITRUS OIL. There are many brands, and you do not need very much of any. For more about this, see page 7.

You will also need a fine mesh strainer, ideally a tamis set with different screens. They are not expensive, but essential tools.

DARK, GOLD AND LIGHT RUMS

These are antiquated terms for reasons that I will explain in detail later (see pages 50-51). Rum enthusiasts have rejected these terms in recent years as being misleading, and rightfully so. They stem from a time when there were very few choices in rum. However, in the broader sense, they are still useful for quickly distinguishing between a rum that is light in flavor compared to one that is heavier and more flavorful.

Black Rum has usually been colored to give the impression that it's older. In some instances, the flavor is not any deeper than some light rums. Black rum may be used for the aesthetics of a cocktail or just for reasons of tradition. **Spiced Rum** is usually to be avoided because flavorings are nearly always added as a way to conceal inferior quality. If you want spices, add them yourself to the cocktail.

THE SOLERA SYSTEM

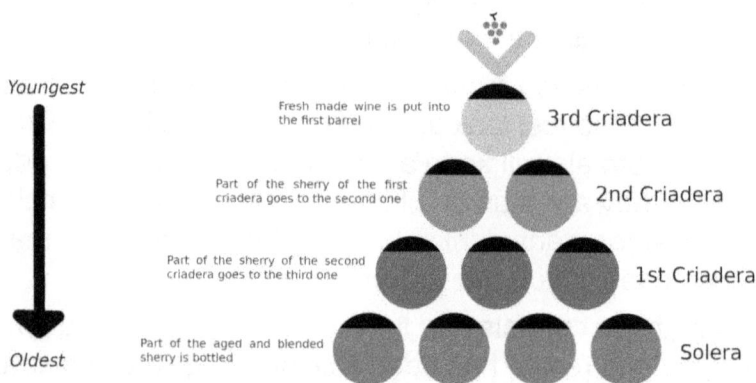

Youngest

Fresh made wine is put into the first barrel — 3rd Criadera

Part of the sherry of the first criadera goes to the second one — 2nd Criadera

Part of the sherry of the second criadera goes to the third one — 1st Criadera

Part of the aged and blended sherry is bottled — Solera

Oldest

Many rums are traditionally aged in casks stacked on top of each other. Solera is the lowest row of casks. A third of the rum in the lowest row is bottled and replaced with rum from the row above it, the first criadera, which is slightly younger. The top row is where the newest rum is introduced. This exact same system is used for sherry and some other aged liquors. Above is a diagram specific for sherry, but the principle is exactly the same for rum. It takes many years for a product to make it all the way through the Solera system barrels to bottling.

DISTILLATION BASICS

Huge books have been written entirely about distillation, so know that this is only a very brief outline of the general processes.

Evaporative Distillation, as it is properly known, relies on the principle that different liquids boil at different temperatures. However, this is an oversimplification already. There are a vast number of *azeotropes*, which are groups of liquids that cannot be separated by distillation alone. An example of this is the mixture of alcohol and water. No matter how carefully you distill this mixture, you can never get rid of about 5% of the water, so other methods have to be used to produce 100% alcohol.

When it comes to mixtures as complicated as liquors, there are countless minor flavor components that are azeotropic mixtures with alcohol, water and each other. So decisions have to be made about what type of still is used and what portion of the distillate to keep, and what portion to discard.

In distillation, vapor rises and gradually the temperature at that point increases as various components then flow through to the cooling (condensation) portion of the still. The first part that comes over is called the *head*. Next comes the *heart*, which is most of the product, and finally the *tail*. Both the head and some of the tail are discarded, as both contain toxic substances as well as not tasting good. The first part of the head is toxic methanol because it boils at the lowest temperature. Naturally, all of that must be discarded.

There are decisions to be made that affect the product. Aside from what temperature range to collect the heart within, there is the important issue of what type of still to use. A column still has perforated baffles that the vapor must pass through like a maze. So it will do a better job of separating components, but if the column is very long, so much heat and time is required that it cooks the ingredients, and this can result in byproducts forming that will carry over as azeotropes. Column stills produce a higher ratio of alcohol.

A shorter path pot still allows for the product to be collected with less heat for a shorter time, but the separation of the head and tail is not as clean. A lot of the head has to be discarded in order to make it safe, but more of what would be left behind in the tail of a column gets included because it hasn't broken down from prolonged and fierce heating. This is why pot still rums and whiskeys are so different from column still products, even if everything else is the same (the same starting material and the same temperature range chosen for the heart fraction).

When it comes to liqueurs, vermouths and digestifs, nearly all are made by distilling alcohol with the fruits, spices and botanicals to obtain one or more concentrates that are then blended together with water, caramel, brandy, wine or some other base ingredient. This provides for reliable reproducible results on a factory scale.

For whiskey, if the bottle says "malt", it has been made in a pot still. If it says "grain", it is nearly always produced in a column still.

Shown here are two small scale "moonshine" stills, but the principles are the same. Commercial stills can be so large that someone can walk around inside to facilitate cleaning.

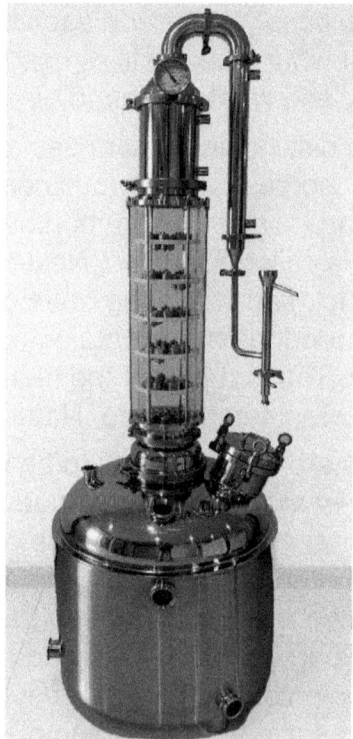

POT STILL   COLUMN STILL

COMMERCIAL LIQUOR DISTILLATION

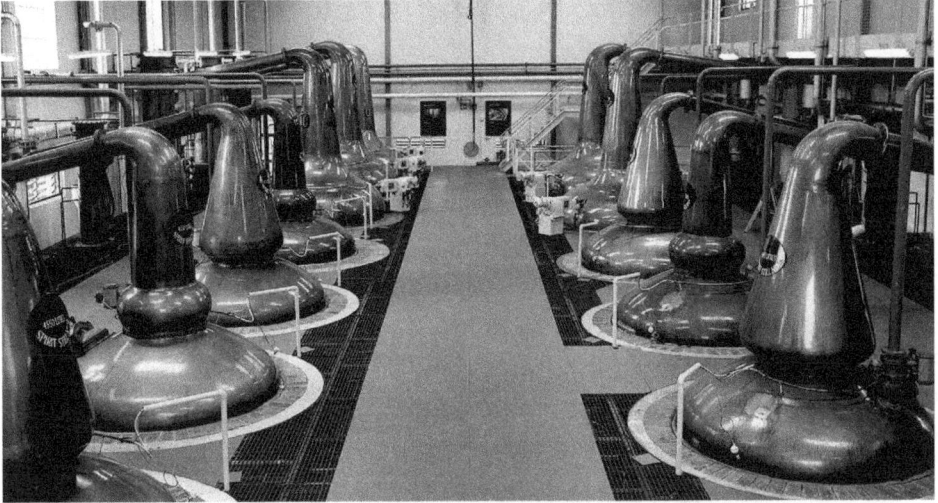

LARGE SCALE POT STILL DISTILLATION

MEDIUM SCALE COLUMN STILL DISTILLATION

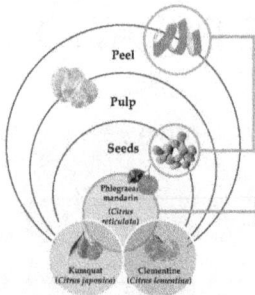

Citrus Fruits and Oils

Citrus fruits contain three individually useful components in mixology: Juice, zest and pith. The outer zest is rich in the oils that define the fruit's individual character.

Just below the zest is the bitter pith. This has less in the way of individual character between citrus fruits, but still the pith of a lime is different in flavor from the pith of an orange. The pith is mostly useful in producing bitter notes. When you squeeze the juice from a citrus fruit, the little specks of membrane you see clouding the juice are similar to the pith. In many cases this is part of the flavor of the cocktail. In other cases, this needs to be strained off to avoid both bitterness and cloudiness. All of the recipes in this book expect that the citrus juice is passed through a regular mesh sieve to remove large bits of pith. Where a recipe states **strained**, it means juice that has also passed through a very fine mesh sieve to remove as much of the solids as possible. Removing the fragments of pith makes the juice more clear as well as reducing the bitter notes of the pith. Sometimes you actually want those notes, so fine mesh straining is not something to do automatically all of the time.

CITRUS OILS

Very few very people are equipped to perform distillation at home, which is normally a critical step in producing commercial liquors and liqueurs. My novel solution to this problem for creating cordials and liqueurs lies in taking advantage of commercially available distilled essential oils (primarily from citrus fruits). This avoids the need for home distillation. Order a set of citrus oils right away!

CITRUS JUICES

Lemons, limes, oranges are all well known ingredients in

cocktails, so they don't warrant an introduction. There are a few points worth mentioning, though. First, all citrus juices need to be either used immediately after squeezing, or refrigerated promptly. They deteriorate rapidly even when in the refrigerator. To convince yourself of this, compare the taste of fresh juice with one that has been refrigerated for just 24 hours.

POMELO: This is the original grapefruit species. They are a bit sweeter and do not have the same sharpness. If you can not get quality white grapefruit, try substituting pomelo juice in cocktails. They do require squeezing by hand and are also rather expensive.

GRAPEFRUIT: There are both pink ("ruby") and "white" grapefruit (which are actually yellow). This distinction is more important in the United States, where pink grapefruit are usually picked green and tend to have unpleasant metallic notes, while white grapefruit are usually of better quality there. There is less difference between pink and white European grapefruit.

YUZU: This Japanese citrus fruit is powerful in both aroma and taste. The fresh fruit is almost never seen outside of Asia, but bottled juice such as the one shown in the photo at the left, is available in better Asian grocery stores and online. Cocktails that are strong with grapefruit notes are sometimes improved by using some yuzu as a sour component because yuzu has many of the same flavor molecules that grapefruits have. However, it can easily overpower other flavors. A little goes a long way. Yuzu pairs well in Japanese sake cocktails, as you might expect.

BERGAMOT: Also known as Bergamot Orange. This is more like a cross between lime, grapefruit and orange in size, color and (to a lesser extent) flavor. This exotic citrus fruit is mostly from southern Italy, though now believed to have originated in Turkey. It is highly fragrant and every bit as unique as Yuzu. The bitters produced from the zest and pith is an excellent and underused cocktail ingredient.

MANDARINES, TANGERINES and SATSUMAS: These varieties of oranges all have their own subtle characteristics and are worth considering when selecting orange juice to use in a new cocktail.

USING CITRUS PEELS AND ZESTS

The technique of grating citrus zest on a sieve and then pouring one or more of the liquors over it was explained in detail in my previous book, so I won't repeat all of that again here. Some recipes in this book make use of that SUPERCHARGING method.

One of the problems many people have is getting citrus fruit peel to expel its natural oil over a cocktail. The problem can be even more daunting when trying to flame the peel. There are three things to do to improve this:

1. Use very fresh citrus fruits. When it is old, the peel will not release oils because it is dry.

2. Keep the fruit that you plan to do this with in the refrigerator until it is cold. That doesn't mean to leave it there for a week, because it will also dry out, but a cold orange (for example) is much easier to make flame than one at room temperature.

3. Slice a deep oval "coin" by cutting in the direction of stem to bottom using a knife (not a vegetable peeler for this). Cutting along the "equator" will produce an inferior piece for this purpose. Cut deep because the zest by itself will not "snap", and that snap is what produces the micro explosion of oils.

After expressing the oil over the top of the cocktail, rub the rim of the glass with it. Also the foot of the glass, if it is stemware. The reason for this is the person drinking it will get the scent on their fingers and as they hold the glass, the warmth of their hands will effuse the aroma of the citrus into their nose.

Finally, if you are going to flame the oils, it is best to use a long butane lighter rather than a small cigarette lighter, or (even worse) a match. This will make it less likely to burn yourself and give you more confidence. A long match that's used to light fireplaces will work, but the aroma of the burnt sulfur is not a pleasant accompaniment to any cocktail.

ICE and DILUTION

There are some myths about which method of cooling a cocktail makes it the coldest, and which method adds the least amount of water to it from the melted ice. After hundreds of carefully conducted experiments, I discovered some interesting facts.

First, no matter how careful one is, there is a surprising amount of variability in the outcome for which there is no easy explanation. Perhaps the exact room temperature at the time, or the precise amount of time between the cooling and the measurement. Tests were conducted using both water and cocktails (more about those ahead). The first tests were conducted with 100ml (3.5 oz) of water and either 90g (3 oz) or 140g (5 oz) of ice (cubes, crushed ice or a single block). The mixture was either stirred or shaken (see below).

AVERAGE RESULTS FOR 100ml (3.5 oz) OF PURE WATER

ICE QUANTITY	METHOD	TEMP °C / °F	DILUTION
90g / 3 oz	Single Block -- Shaken	8.0°C / 46°F	16ml / 0.6 oz
90g / 3 oz	Single Block -- Stirred	7.5°C / 45°F	16ml / 0.6 oz
90g / 3 oz	Cubes -- Shaken	2.3°C / 36°F	35ml / 1.2 oz
140g / 5 oz	Cubes -- Shaken	2.5°C / 38°F	31ml / 1.1 oz
90g / 3 oz	Cubes -- Stirred	3.5°C / 38°F	28ml / 0.9 oz
140g / 5 oz	Cubes -- Stirred	2.7°C / 37°F	23ml / 0.8 oz
90g / 3 oz	Crushed Ice -- Shaken	2.0°C / 36°F	41ml / 1.4 oz
140g / 5 oz	Crushed Ice -- Shaken	2.2°C / 36°F	30ml / 1.1 oz

Curiously, no matter how carefully tests were conducted, results could not be reproduced to more than plus or minus about one degree Celsius, and the amount of dilution could not be reproduced

10

closer than +/- 5 milliliters (about 1 teaspoon). The starting temperature of the water (or cocktail) was 22°C (71.6°F) for all tests. Stirring was 60 stirs with a bar spoon. Shaking was 20 times. All tests were double-strained to remove any ice chips.

The most extreme difference was between the tests with water vs. the tests with a cocktail (or plain vodka). Alcohol gets colder and also results in much more dilution across all tests. For example, as you can see in the table on the opposite page, stirring 100ml (3.5 oz) of water with 90 grams (3 oz) of ice cubes, the resulting temperature was 3.5°C (38°F). When the same experiment was performed with a Negroni, the temperature was down to nearly 0°C (32°F), but it took on 36ml of water from the melted ice (more than 8ml additional, or 1/4 ounce).

Repeating this test with 140 grams (5 oz) of ice cubes, plain water was 2.7°C (37°F), while the Negroni temperature was 0.7°C (33°C) and it had taken on a huge 15ml (1/2 oz) of water.

CONCLUSIONS

The old counter-intuitive bartender belief that adding *more* ice cubes to the shaker will result in *less* dilution has been confirmed— but only when chilling down pure water! As soon as alcohol enters the picture, **more ice means more dilution**.

Not surprisingly, a single block of ice results in less dilution and less cooling. At least not right away. The single large block of ice in a cocktail will continue to bring the temperature down without diluting it very quickly. This is very often the best choice, especially for those who slowly sip their drinks.

The other factor to consider when deciding which method to use is how the cocktail behaves in terms of temperature and dilution straight up vs. with a single large block of ice, or with ice cubes, or with crushed ice. The answer is exactly what you would probably guess. No ice = no dilution but fastest in warming up. At the opposite end of that spectrum is crushed ice, which keeps the drink cold the longest, but dilutes it the most and the fastest.

✦

COCKTAIL BITTERS

In cocktails, bitters can be thought of as being similar to how spices are used in cooking. They can enhance almost everything when used in the right amount. There is one important rule that is all too often ignored: **DO NOT SUBSTITUTE BITTERS.** In cooking, that would be like swapping pepper for cinnamon. It won't end well.

Originally bitters were marketed and used as medicines. but by the late 19th Century they were being widely used in cocktails. The three best known at the time were Angostura, Boker's and to a somewhat lesser extent, Peychaud's.

ANGOSTURA BITTERS

Johann Siegert, a German doctor working in Venezuela around 1820, learned about various herbal medicines from natives of the Amazon rainforest. Among these was a treatment for stomach pains, which he began marketing around 1824 as Angostura. The name means "narrowing" in Spanish, referring to the place where the river nearby narrowed. This is confusing because there is also an angostura plant *(Angostura trifoliata)* native to the same region of South America. The bark of this also has medicinal properties, being used by natives to treat fevers. The exact formula of Angostura Bitters is a secret, but one thing we do know is that it does not contain any of that *Angostura trifoliata* plant. Occasionally you find imitators that actually do include *Angostura trifoliata* in order to legally call their product *Angostura Bitters*, taking advantage of a loophole in copyright law since one is a brand name and the other is an ingredient that is coincidentally the same word.

Sailors would purchase Angostura Bitters to keep with them for stomach ailments, and it wasn't long before they began mixing it with various liquors. The number of cocktails that call for Angostura Bitters today is encyclopedic. A principle ingredient is gentian root, and if you want to taste that by itself, try Suze Gentian liqueur.

In 1875 the factory was relocated to the island of Trinidad, where it resides to this day. While most cocktails call for only a very small amount of Angostura, these bitters have became very popular in Trinidad, where they are often drank straight over ice. Then there is the Trinidad Sour cocktail that calls for a whopping 45ml (1.5 oz) of Angostura Bitters per cocktail.

One other interesting fact is that the label on the bottle that extends up too high was originally a mistake when the printing company accidentally made them too large. To meet their order requests, they decided to just use them as they were, leaving the excess paper protruding up. This became popular and so they decided to purposely make that part of their brand's appearance. In 2007 when the company introduced Angostura Orange Bitters, they followed the same design with an oversize label, too.

ORANGE BITTERS

These days there are a staggering array of bitters sold in just about every flavor profile imaginable. Many have very limited use and most are quite expensive. In modern cocktails, the two most important kinds are Angostura and orange bitters. There are three brands of orange bitters that I strongly recommend.

1. **Fee Bros. Orange Bitters**. *This has a strong fresh orange taste. It is rather sweet as bitters go.*

2. **Angostura Orange Bitters**. *Very well balanced and more complex than other orange bitters. More bitter than Fee Bros., but not in an unpleasant way.*

3. **Scrappy's Seville Orange Bitters**. *The taste of the bitter rind dominates. This ingredient can sometimes be replaced by grating orange zest onto a sieve and pouring liquor over it, as explained in my previous cocktail book. Also note that Scrappy's makes a regular (not Seville) orange bitters, which are similar to the Angostura Orange bitter product but a bit lacking in complexity.*

BOKER'S BITTERS

This was so beloved by famous 19th Century mixologist, Jerry Thomas, that he put it in almost every cocktail he created. He stated that he prefered it to Angostura. Boker's original formula was lost when the company went out of business due to Prohibition in the 1920's. Then someone found an old bottle in the early 2000's and chemists went to work to analyze that sample. The established dominant ingredients are cardamom, cinnamon and orange peel.

The reverse engineered recipe was circulated and now several manufactures produce a version of it. If you are attempting to make one of Jerry Thomas' recipes, then this is the best you can hope for in terms of authenticity. However, personally I find it is only useful occasionally.

PEYCHAUD'S BITTERS

Created in 1830 by a Haitian pharmacist in New Orleans, Like Angostura, Peychaud's is also primarily flavored by gentian, but it is less aggressive and more floral. There are notes of anise and mint. Relatively few cocktail recipes specifically call for this ingredient, with the notable exception of the Louisiana cocktail, the Sazerac.

OTHER BITTERS

All bitters are worth experimenting with, but a large collection of them is expensive. The ones that I consider most essential for a serious cocktail enthusiast are Angostura, all three orange bitters mentioned on the previous page, and the following:

Grapefruit Bitters, Fee Bros. and/or Scrappy's (grapefruit zest)

Elemakule Tiki Bitters, Bittermens (spices)

Xocolatl Mole Bitters, Bittermens (chocolate, spices, mild heat)

Aztec Chocolate Bitters, Fee Bros. (dark bitter chocolate)

Cardamom Bitters, Fee Bros. (cardamom spice)

Black Walnut Bitters, Fee Bros. (deep nutty taste)

Bergamot Bitters, Miracle Mile (bergamot zest)

MAKING YOUR OWN BITTERS

The main problem is obtaining key ingredients for classic bitter recipes, such as chinchona bark, callamus root and many exotic plants. Also, most commercial recipes require distillation, or even vacuum distillation, which is even more impractical for individuals.

The other issue is that many bitters require extensive aging. Sometimes for years, which isn't usually something people want to take on. With that in mind, note that a recipe for Bergamot Bitters is on page 204.

OTHER BITTER FLAVORS

The bitter component of a cocktail is not always from dashes of bitters *per se*, but often the inclusion of a bitter apertif. Bitter flavors are an acquired taste because bitterness is biologically our taste sensation warning us of a poisonous plant or substance. This sense has been with us for millions of years, so overcoming it has been compared to enjoying spicy hot chilies. It's not for everyone, but many people *really* enjoy it.

There are two primary plant sources of bitterness in bitter apertifs and amari. One of these is gentian, which is the dried and aged roots of several related flowering plant that grow high in the French and Swiss Alps. Curiously, the chemical responsible for its bitter taste only develops after drying and aging the roots.

The other frequent source of bitterness is Cinchona, which is the bark of a tree. It looks like cinnamon, but tastes nothing like it. This is what tonic water is flavored with. Although quinine is the main source of the bitterness, it also has other complex flavors. Historically it has been used as a medicine for malaria as well as many other ailments. Like most of those antiquated herbal remedies, they relied either partly or entirely on the placebo effect.

In his book, *Principles of Orchestration*, famed Russian composer Rimsky-Korsakov (best known for The Flight of the Bumblebee), made a brilliant observation about the stages that a young composer goes through. Initially they fall in love with the string section, because when a sea of violins and cellos are playing, even a rather poor arrangement with some foul chords still sounds acceptable because the audience is mostly hearing the beauty of the instruments rather than the music itself. In cocktails, this is the sugar effect. With enough sweetener, virtually any combination of ingredients will be palatable. In fact, the concept of sweet drinks was largely born during Prohibition when foul tasting moonshine could only be stomached with very sweet syrups.

The next stage for a composer is a love affair with cymbals because the long lasting white noise of each crash covers up dissonance. In cocktails, the parallel is adding cream, or often in the case of Tiki drinks, coconut cream. A little goes a long way.

Another tool of the novice to smooth everything over, is excessive dilution. This may be by the addition of a large volume of soda water, or by blending a cocktail with a lot of ice. If you combine these three sins together for a cocktail that is very sweet, very creamy and very dilute, and you have what is known as a real "girly drink" (although such sexism is frowned upon these days, I know). The watered down Piña Colada served in most restaurants is a perfect example of this. Of course, if that's what you like, then enjoy. Just realize that this is considered the kindergarten level of mixology because it doesn't take a bartender to make a flavored milkshake, and that's what you have with sugar, cream and ice.

The final stage of the composer is when their composition harmonizes in such a way that the mind is imagining a melody that is written between the lines, so to speak. The music can be heard in a different way each time depending on what you are paying attention to and your mood. This is the same goal to strive for in creating a cocktail. This is the result of different flavors hitting your palate spaced apart slightly due to how your senses process the different flavor molecules in the cocktail. Some take longer to register than others, but it is not quite that simple because the time will vary with other ingredients present, as well as the temperature of the drink and the dilution. The drink must be balanced overall, too (of course). Simply bombarding one's senses with several waves of incompatible flavors is about the worst thing possible. To use a musical analogy once again, that's like calling the sound of a jackhammer being drowned out by a screaming baby "music". I have put together a simple guide for how to land in the ballpark of a new and delicious cocktail using a novel formula in a later chapter here (begins on page 59).

The point is that a bitter component is nearly always required to achieve both balance and the sophistication of flavors arriving in waves. The bitter component rarely plays a prominent melody (except in drinks like a Negroni), but without any bitter component, cocktails usually taste one-dimensional. Even a few drops can alter flavor perceptions in amazing ways. If you absolutely hate anything bitter, then try to expand your palate gradually because this is rather like hating any spices in food. If you bought this book, it must be assumed you aren't the sort of person who lives only for watered down Piña Coladas. Presumably you have already graduated from that early stage and are ready for something more adventurous.

Bitter Apertifs and Digestifs

There are five broad categories of bitter components used in mixing cocktails. Those are:

1. Cocktail Bitters
These are the most intense bitter flavors in small dropper bottles such as Angostura.

2. Apertifs and Digestifs
Common examples include Campari and Aperol.

3. Amari
Bitter apertifs with a higher alcohol concentration that were traditionally made in Italy. Note that Amari is the plural of Amaro.

4. Vermouth
Wines with sugar or caramel that have been infused with herbs and bitter components macerated in alcohol.

5. Tonic Water
Sparkling water infused with either synthetic quinine or cinchona bark (which is where natural quinine comes from).

All of these were originally intended as medicines, including tonic water. Eventually they became popular to consume for the taste. By the 19th century, bartenders found that these could be enjoyed when mixed with other spirits. There is no fixed rule for what makes something an apertif (meaning *before the meal*) vs. what makes something a digestive (*after the meal*). All were originally sold as being suitable for either, with the idea that a larger drink with ice or soda (and a low alcohol content) was an apertif, and a smaller cocktail with a higher alcohol content was a digestive.

But what makes something a bitter apertif, or an amaro, or a vermouth, and not either one of the other two? Campari runs a master class for professionals in which technical questions are answered. Before I could ask this question, others already had, because it is so frequently pondered by bartenders. Their answer was accurate, but not very satisfying. Namely, many products simply defy classification in any one category. Take for example Punt E Mes, which is widely regarded as a very potent but sweet vermouth. Yet it was intended as a bitter apertif (it says so right on the label), and marketed as such on up to the 1980's.

One of the most confusing bitter liquors of all is Cynar (memorable for the giant artichoke on the label). This is halfway between a vermouth and a bitter apertif such as Campari, and was marketed as a digestive in the 1960's and 1970's.

Until recently, at least Amari could be categorized as Italian bitter liqueurs with formulas dating back more than a century, Nearly all have 30 to 40% alcohol. Now there are products being called Amari from other parts of the world such as Amaro Di Angostura from Trinidad. As if all of that isn't confusing enough, Australia has recently entered the game with dozens of vermouths and bitter apertifs that are all over the map in terms of alcohol, sugar and bitterness. An entire book could be written about those alone, except that most of those products will be discontinued soon, and many are not even distributed outside of Australia.

So how does one make sense of this? You just have to accept there is a broad spectrum of bitter components with different manufacturers trying to market them in different ways. Just as in the 19th century when none of these things were intended to be part of a cocktail and sold only as remedies, your creativity in applying them should not be constrained by what the manufacturer says it's for. If we followed the original 19th century manufacturer's directions, we would be drinking Coca-Cola for stomach aches.

Sugar Analysis

The amount of sugar in some of these products—the ones sold in Finland—has been analyzed and made public, as per Finnish law. The sugar content listed here is from Finnish government data.

Campari (25% Alcohol, 25% Sugar)

Campari is an alcoholic spirit obtained from the infusion of bitter herbs, aromatic plants and fruits in alcohol, which describes pretty much every apertif, amaro and vermouth. Of course the difference lies in the specific recipe. Also, as is the case with nearly all such spirits, alcohol and water are the only ingredients in their secret recipe that the company will admit to. However, it has been leaked over the years that some of the ingredients include cherry tree bark, the root of rhubarb (not the stalks), and the dried peels of citrus fruits. Based on the flavor, there is a very strong chance that it contains ginseng, wormwood, angelica and camphor. It is named for the originator, Gaspare Campari, and not for the camphor aroma.

The intense red color and sharp distinctive bitter taste make it extremely recognizable, and a key ingredient of some iconic cocktails such as the Negroni. In the world of Tiki, the classic Jungle Bird is based on Campari. This is often regarded as a litmus test for how experienced or adventurous a person is with cocktail culture, because humans have a natural aversion to bitter flavors (as covered in the introduction to this section). If you enjoy some bitter flavors and can differentiate between them, then your options are much broader for the enjoyment of cocktails from around the world.

Aperol (11% Alcohol except Germany with 15%, 25% Sugar)

Although Aperol was originally made by a separate company, now it is part of the Campari group. Some of the ingredients are known to be the same, but Aperol is not as bitter and has a strong hit of bitter orange peel in the nose and initial taste. That quickly fades into syrup and woody notes and finally ends with a soft lingering bitterness and some faint cinnamon.

Cynar (16.5% Alcohol, 26% Sugar)

Although the key ingredient is artichokes, which are naturally bitter, there is no detectable artichoke flavor in it. Even though this is often referred to as a bitter apertif, it is more like a cross between sweet vermouth and an amaro. Consequently, it is a bit more difficult to pair in cocktails because it is like adding two ingredients at the same time, and you don't have control ovor the ratio of them.

Fernet Branca (39% Alcohol, 25% Sugar)

This one is extremely bitter and somewhat acrid. Although some people do drink it straight or on the rocks, it is very much an acquired taste. To the uninitiated, it is reminiscent of burning rubber. Even if you don't like it straight, it can be used as a bitter in cocktails, particularly with bourbon and whiskey. Fernet Branca is so potent that it easily overpowers most flavors.

Suze Gentian Liqueur (15% Alcohol in France, 20% Export)

This French product is much less bitter than most of the others listed here.

The only known ingredient is gentian root, as you would expect from the name, but there are strong floral notes and a long complicated finish. The amount of sugar is not published, but it is low (probably 10% or less).

Gammel Dansk (38% Alcohol, 7% Sugar)

This Danish bitter apertif is uncommon outside of Europe, but worth seeking out. A major component is Rowan (also known as Mountain Ash), which is a fruit that's quite astringent, which is an unusual character among apertifs and digestifs. There are 29 herbs, spices and flowers in this secret recipe. The more tame middle notes are caraway and cumin, tapering off to something similar to Peychaud's bitters for an extremely long and bone dry finish. The name translates to "Old Danish".

Underberg (44% Alcohol, 3% Sugar)

A German product. Generally sold in very small bottles intended to be consumed as a single portion at one time. Very low sugar. Although rarely called for in cocktail recipes, this is a useful bitter component.

Galliano L'Apertivo (24% Alcohol, 19% Sugar)

Not to be confused with other Galliano products. Thinner and more bitter than Campari, but seemingly based on the same flavor profile. There are additional notes from classic Galliano including anise, orange and grapefruit peels, vanilla and a hit of black pepper in the aftertaste.

Amaro Family

The defining differences between a bitter apertif or digestive and an amaro is that the latter is generally higher in alcohol and not quite as bitter. Although traditionally amari only came from Italy, other countries now produce similar liqueurs that they call amari. Some products defy classification, such as Zwack from Hungary.

Amaro Montenegro (23% Alcohol, 26% Sugar)

From Bologna, Italy, this is a secret recipe with botanicals imported from around the world. The production process is unusually complex with the botanicals being divided into six subgroups, each macerated and distilled separately before being mixed together to taste. The flavor is quite complex with notes of lavender, vanilla, lemon peel and green ferns. The latter element is what defines it. Of course there is also caramel and wormwood. Even though the sugar content is in the normal range for an amaro, it comes across as sweeter than most.

Amaro Averna (29% Alcohol, 22% Sugar)

While the initial flavors are coffee and cola, the defining subtle secondary notes that arrive later on your palate are (sequentially) raspberries, celery and finally, much later, honeydew melon. I don't know if any of those are actual ingredients because the recipe of this Sicilian amaro is also a secret.

Bigallet China China (40% Alcohol, 26% Sugar)

The single defining flavor of this is burnt orange peel, but not in an unpleasant way. From the company's description: "Produced by Bigallet since 1875, China China is a bitter liqueur obtained from macerated and distilled orange peels blended with a bouquet of aromatic and spicy plants." The bitterness comes from wormwood, as usual. Unusual and excellent.

Vecchio Amaro del Capo (35% Alcohol, 25% Sugar)

Strong notes of pine, cloves and black pepper with the same quinine as in tonic water. There is a rapid rise and fall of caramel sweetness that is overtaken by brief mandarine orange, giving way to some alcohol burn. Finally only the quinine is left behind on your palate.

Amaro Nonino (35% Alcohol, 25% Sugar)

Based on grappa. Infused with all three of the big bitter components: cinchona, gentian root and wormwood, yet it is not nearly as bitter as Fernet Branca. It is also infused with thyme. It is unusual among amari for being aged in oak barrels for five years. The subtle flavor profile is oranges, cinnamon, apricots and caramel with a hint of saffron in the finish.

Ramazzotti Amaro (30% Alcohol, 25% Sugar)

Made with 33 different herbs including gentian. Berry and bitter orange notes in the aroma and taste with a long slow finish with star anise, cardamom, nuts and a hint of coffee. First created in 1815 in Milan, Italy.

Amaro di Angostura (35% Alcohol)

Not a true amaro since it comes from Trinidad by the maker of Angostura bitters. The primary flavors are dark cherries, root beer, cinnamon and cloves. The bitterness comes from gentian root. It pairs best with rums.

Nardini l'Amaro (31% Alcohol, 22% Sugar)

After being featured in the television series, *The Sopranos*, this previously seldom-seen amaro import became a best seller. As for flavor, it's a case of "the usual suspects" of licorice, orange zest, spices and mint backing up gentian and wormwood bitterness. There are dozens of Italian amari, most of which are rarely seen elsewhere, and all are variations on a theme.

Balsam

The following amari are known to contain balsam (some other bitter apertifs may also contain balsam, but that would be part of their secret ingredients). Balsam is the sap from a tree with a unique earthy vanilla and tree bark taste. It is an important ingredient in many perfumes, and also in this type of bitter digestif.

Poli Vaca Mora Amaro (32% Alcohol, 20% Sugar)

This is an Italian amaro that is produced by infusing grappa, unlike most amari that are based on grain alcohol. The nose is strong with eucalyptus. The taste is a mixture of licorice, mint and caramel that fades to an extremely long lingering taste of eucalyptus. It also contains balsam, but as usual, the recipe is a guarded secret.

Riga Black Balsam (45% Alcohol)

From Latvia since 1752, this is older than most Italian amari (possibly older than any Italian amaro, in fact). The primary flavors are birch, berries, ginger, peppermint and nutmeg. While virtually all amari contain wormwood (of which there are at least five species used in bitter liquors), Riga Black Balsam is unusual for including the same type of wormwood used in producing absinthe, which is almost never used in any other product but absinthe. It comes in a dark brown ceramic bottle. There are also purple and red versions that are strong with black current and cherry flavors, respectively. The fruity versions have a lower alcohol content of 30%.

Balsam Bitters from Belarus

For the sake of completeness, I should mention that bitters of this sort are very popular in the former Soviet nation of Belarus. As far as I know, none of them are exported, which is unfortunate because many of them are unique in flavor from local botanicals. *Black Queen* is especially delicious.

Quinquinas & Americanos

These are in a family that straddles the line between amaro and vermouth. *Amer* in this case means bitter, and has nothing to do with America, the country. Americanos get their bitterness from gentian root. Quinquina (pronounced *ken-key-nah*) is bitter from cinchona bark as a source of quinine (the same ingredient that makes tonic water bitter). Notable examples of these include:

Lillet Blanc (17% Alcohol, 9% Sugar)

An infused white wine with slight bitterness and soft orange notes.

Lillet Rosé (17% Alcohol, 7% Sugar)

An infused rosé wine with slight bitterness and soft grapefruit notes.

Cocchi Americano (16.5% Alcohol, 20% Sugar)

An infused and sweetened white wine with notes of wild flowers and faint citrus.

Dubonnet (Currently: 14.8% Alcohol, 16% Sugar)

Originally 21% alcohol. Dubonnet has a complicated history with the recipe having been changed several times and the rights to production sold to an American company many years ago, which produces a different version from the European Dubonnet. It is a fortified wine made with grape juice, herbs and quinine. Because the recipe has been altered so many times, keep in mind that any older cocktail recipe calling for it will come out different than was originally intended.

Vermouth

Not that many years ago this was a very simple topic, especially when it came to vermouth in cocktails. There were only two types ever called for: Italian (sweet) vermouth and French (dry) vermouth. Of course there were several brands of each, but no emphasis was put on the brand in recipes. Today there is a dizzying variety of different vermouths made in many different countries, many of which are not even vermouth in terms of classic flavor profiles. Originally all vermouth had to contain wormwood as the bitter component. In fact, the very name vermouth is derived from the German word for wormwood, *vormat*. While wormwood is mostly famous for supposedly causing hallucinations in Absinthe (see page 34 for more about Absinthe), it does not. More to the point, there are several different species of wormwood and vermouths are seldom made with the same type of wormwood than Absinthe is.

These days there are many products on the market sold as vermouth that do not contain any wormwood at all, but they do contain some other bitter components. This has made the topic even more confusing. Most white wine vermouths are dark reddish brown either because of caramel or because of other dark colored botanicals in them. Furthermore, these days vermouths are sometimes made from rosé wines, or even a blend of red and white wines. There are very few rules.

All vermouths are a mixture of three components: Wine, sugar (or caramel) and a botanical infusion. The latter is usually produced separately from a mixture of herbs and spices in alcohol that is distilled. Some of the flavors of those botanicals are concentrated in the distillate. Then this is added to the wine and sugar mix in the right proportion. All vermouths have an alcohol concentration a bit stronger than wine, averaging around 18% by volume.

These days some vermouths macerate the botanicals directly with the wine in the same scheme that was used to make bathtub gin back in the days of Prohibition. The true origin of vermouths goes back to ancient China and Egypt where the "bathtub" maceration method was all they knew how to do because distillation hadn't been invented yet.

The bottom line is that the world of vermouths now is a vast and confusing landscape of flavors and qualities—some worthy artisanal creations and some mass produced rotgut. Many of these are intended to be drank directly over ice. When it comes to cocktails, it still comes down to dry white or sweet red.

While manufacturers and purists will tell you that vermouths should be stored refrigerated and consumed soon after opening, this is rarely the case in practice. I have never known a bar to refrigerate its vermouth, and I defy anyone to taste the difference in a cocktail between a freshly opened bottle and one that is several months old (providing it was kept out of direct sunlight and at normal room temperature). So save your refrigerator space for other things. You'll need it when you get further along in this book!

Dry Vermouth

Generally speaking, any recipe that calls for a dry vermouth (or French vermouth in older recipes) is going to be easy to satisfy because there is not as much variety among dry vermouths, especially if you stick to well known brands such as Noilly Pratt, Dolin or Martini & Rossi. Just be sure it is labeled *dry* and not *bianco* or *blanco*. These are a sweet white vermouth that is not well suited to most cocktails.

Sweet Vermouth

Long ago, this style came entirely from Italy, so the term Italian Vermouth became synonymous with Sweet Vermouth. While most people assume these are made from red wines, nearly all are made from white wines and colored with caramel and sometimes other ingredients. They range in intensity between lighter and more fruity to dark and deep. These days there are dozens of sweet vermouths from Italy as well as some from other countries. It would be pointless to even try to list them all, especially since the majority of them are not exported. Here are some of the representative sweet vermouths most commonly used in cocktail making today:

Antica Formula (16.5% Alcohol, 19% Sugar)

This is the original vermouth and still respected as a true masterpiece. It is deep, rich and complex. Rest assured that any recipe that specifies this vermouth is not going to be improved by any other vermouth in its place.

Martini & Rossi *Rosso* (15% Alcohol, 15% Sugar)

Arguably the most famous brand of vermouth in the world today. They produce both a dry white and a red (rosso) variety in addition to some types that are intended for consuming straight over ice. Their Rosso vermouth is often used as a benchmark for what a middle-of-the road light Italian sweet vermouth is expected to taste like. There are notes of nutmeg, licorice and cola that make it more popular than it really deserves to be. Few cocktails are improved by this choice of vermouth over other available options.

Cinzano *Rosso* (15% Alcohol, 15% Sugar)

Unlike most sweet vermouths, this is actually made from red wine, although it still has caramel added that enhances the color and sweetness. It is infused with a secret blend of more than 30 botanical ingredients. The subtle astringent tannins from the red wine give this its unique profile. The aftertaste has notes of orange bitters.

Tosti *Rosso* (14.7% Alcohol, 15% Sugar)

An exceptional value for a workhorse vermouth that functions perfectly well in most cocktails that specify only a generic sweet Italian vermouth in their recipe. Preferable to both Cinzano and Martini & Rossi in most cases.

Cocchi Vermouth di Torino (16% Alcohol, 20% Sugar)

As of 2011, this Italian D.O.C. product was restored to the original formula dating back over a century. The ingredients include spices that are faintly reminiscent of curry powder, as well as the "usual suspects" of quinine, citrus peel, roots and mint. Note that it has more sugar than most other sweet vermouths.

Punt E Mes (16% Alcohol, 22% Sugar)

The name means "point and a half", which is in reference to it being one and a half times as bitter as Carpano's Antica Formula vermouth (which is often chosen as the benchmark for bitterness among sweet vermouths). Despite the relatively high sugar content, the bitterness conceals the sweetness when you sample it directly, but it will come through in a cocktail.

Fortified Wines

I'm going to ignore the vast topics of ordinary red and white wines. If you are reading this book, it must be assumed you already have a fundamental understanding of what wines are. When it comes to mixology, red wine is basically only used in Sangria and a few old fashioned punch bowls. White wine is also rare as an ingredient in cocktails as such. Of course wine is the basis of many other spirits such as Cognac and Vermouth, but those are covered elsewhere in this book.

Vincotto

One peculiar wine ingredient that bears mentioning. Vincotto is an Italian product made by the slow reduction of either wine or the juices that would be used to produce wine, until it is a thick sweet syrup. While this is certainly not a common ingredient in cocktails, it should be more so. If you are looking for a unique flavor to craft a novel cocktail, this is well worth seeking out. If you can't find it, you can make your own.

Sherry

All sherries are made in the Jerez region in southern Spain. The alcohol concentration runs between 17 and 20% with only a few rare exceptions. Sugar is extremely variable, from nearly zero on up to 40% or even more. There are several principle classifications:

Fino is a dry (very low sugar) sherry that is aged under a layer of yeast that protects it from the air. It is intended to be drank chilled and neat within a few days of opening the bottle. However, it actually has a long shelf life for cocktails.

Manzanilla is a Fino sherry produced only in Sanlucar de Barrameda, Spain. This is a seaside location and the salt air has some *terroir* effect on the grapes and process.

Amontillado is a Fino that has been aged, but with a barrier of yeast protecting it from oxygen. It is darker, richer and nuttier than Fino, but still rather dry.

Palo Cortado is often produced by accident. It was intended to be a Fino or Amontillado, but something unknown went wrong and the layer of protective yeast broke down, causing it to spend part of its time aging like an Oloroso. Since it became a sought-after commodity, some is manufactured by destroying the protective yeast layer intentionally after 3-4 years of aging. However, the Palo Cortada that happens by random chance can be valuable and sought after.

Oloroso is aged without any protective yeast layer. It is much darker and sweeter. Oloroso is divided according to how sweet it is, being dry, medium or **Cream Sherry**. The latter is not aged as long and may have sugar or caramel added.

Pedro Ximénez is produced from grapes of the same name. Like Italian Amarone wine, the grapes are dried in the sun like raisins to concentrate the sugars. Thus, Pedro Ximénez sherries are extremely sweet, sometimes to the point of being syrupy. Lustau's *San Emilio* is 42% sugar!

Finally, sherries are aged different lengths of time, but the exact time is almost never specified. Just as cognac has vague aging times such as *VS,* etc., sherry has the designations *VOS* (at least 20 years old) and *VORS* (30 years or older). Sherry does not continue to age in the bottle. Unless otherwise specified, anytime sherry is called for in a cocktail, your best bet is a medium Oloroso.

Like other fortified wines, most Sherry will remain perfectly useable in cocktails and for cooking at least 3 months after opening the bottle, provided it is kept cool and out of direct sunlight.

Madeira

Madeira is another example of a very useful cocktail ingredient that is seldom called for, but should be. In actually used to be quite common in the 1800's. Famed mixologist Jerry Thomas had several cocktails based on Madeira, but it went out of style. The extended period in which Madeira was unavailable during Prohibition is the likely reason why it was forgotten. There are a few Madeira cocktails in this book (see the Index at the back). Madeira has a complex and rich flavor and integrates beautifully with rum, cognac, applejack, Calvados and whiskey (although it does not play very well with vodka or Scotch).

The history of Madeira is quite unusual. It was named after a port where ships would pick up barrels of ordinary local wine for sea voyages. Round trips could last years back then in the 1600's. The ship's holds (where the barrels were stored) were hot and steamy much of the time. When barrels of the wine sometimes returned back to Spain, it was discovered that they had aged in a remarkable way. Barrels that had made the "Round Trip" and marked as such, commanded a high price for their special flavor. The Spanish soon set about duplicating these conditions without needing to transport the barrels around the world. They heated the wine between 46° and 55°C (115° to 130°F) for months, which is called the "Estufagem" process. That's how Madeira is still made.

There are three basic divisions. The least expensive is produced in stainless steel or concrete vats fitted with a pipe to heat the wine continuously for about half a year. The better grade is set in barrels and heated outdoors in the hot Spanish summer sun. The best grade is set in barrels in what amounts to a steamy sauna and kept for a year or even longer with the maintenance of heat and steam. Originally performed with manual labor (people stoking the fires in shifts around the clock), but now the process is controlled by computers that monitor humidity and temperature.

There is another peculiarity of Madeira. That is, the types of grapes used are broadly separated into two categories and there are different rules for each type. The grapes in the superior "noble" group are Sercial, Verdelho, Bual, Malvasia and Terrantez. The age further defines Madeira, as described on the label.

Finest is, ironically, the lowest grade and only really suitable for cooking with. Although personally I wouldn't cook with it.

Reserve contains at least 85% of the noble variety of grapes and is aged 5 years. Good for both cocktails and cooking.

Special Reserve has been aged 10 years.

Extra Reserve has been aged 15 years.

Vintage or **Frasqueira** has been aged at least 19 years in barrels and another year in the bottle, so it is 20 years old minimum. These are rare and quite expensive, generally in the hundreds of dollars (or euros) per bottle, or more.

When it comes to cocktails, the *Reserve* level is generally as far as you need to go because the subtle differences beyond that are likely to be buried beneath the other ingredients. An opened bottle will remain perfectly fine for cocktails and for cooking for at least three months, and often six.

Port

This is another fortified wine, meaning the fermentation was stopped by killing the yeast with the addition of alcohol. Although it is commonly said that brandy is added in that phase, this is not really true. There is a distilled grape alcohol used, but it is quite different from either brandy or grappa.

The name comes from the port city of Porto on the Douro river in Portugal. In the European Union, only port wines from that region are legally allowed to be called Port. In other parts of the world, this rule is often ignored.

There are dozens of grape varieties that are legally used to produce Port, including both red and white grapes. However, nearly all port is made using one or more of just five varieties, so there is a lot of similarity in the basic flavor profiles between ports. Like Sherry, there are subtypes of Port:

Ruby is the least expensive and most widely produced type of Port. It is almost always aged in concrete or steel tanks. The flavor is sweet, bright and full of berry notes. When a cocktail recipe calls for Port, this is the default choice.

Tawny Port is produced from red grape varieties and aged in wood barrels. These are more brown in color and can be quite sweet, depending on the age and methods used. They are generally a dessert wine and seldom called for in cocktail recipes.

Late Bottle Vintage (LBV) This should not be confused with late harvest wines such as zinfandels. This style began as lesser quality Port that did not sell and was left behind in barrels much longer than intended (4 to 6 years). They are not as refined as Vintage Port (see below) but offer value. They come in two types: Filtered and Unfiltered. The Filtered are ready to drink as soon as they are opened. The Unfiltered need to be decanted and then rested for at least a couple of hours. This type should be drank within a few days after opening.

Vintage Ports are first aged in either steel tanks or barrels for about two years before being bottled. Then they continue to age in the bottle for at least 10 years, and 40 years is not uncommon. They continue to gain complexity with time. Again, these are basically never used in cocktails.

White Port is produced from white grapes, as one would expect. After Ruby, this is the most common Port to use in cocktails. These range between semi-dry and very sweet. Sometimes White Ports are aged in wood barrels for an extended time, which causes them to darken in color, but they are still called White. After decades they can be as dark as stout beer. Unless stated otherwise, any recipe calling for White Port means a younger one, not vintage.

The common belief that Port needs to be consumed soon after opening the bottle seems to be a fable told by those producing and selling Port (with the exception of fine vintage Port, which actually should be consumed within a few days after opening). Ruby and White Port are extremely stable at room temperature after being opened. There are many stories of half finished bottles of Port found left for ten years or more that were still perfectly fine. This is even more the case if you are mixing cocktails with them.

Prohibition Port is an imitation invented during Prohibition. It is a blend of red wine, red grape juice, simple sugar syrup and 120-proof Everclear (or 80-proof vodka, but that's not as good). The exact proportions vary with the red wine used, but approximately 3:1:1:1. As you might expect, this is especially successful as a faux Port when used in vintage punch bowl recipes with fruit.

HERBAL COMPONENTS

Herbal notes in a cocktail are generally derived from the inclusion of an herbal liqueur, although occasionally fresh herbs are muddled in, such as the mint in a Mojito.

Some important herbal liqueurs include:

D.O.M. Benedictine (40% Alcohol, 36% Sugar)

Created in France in the mid-19th century. Arguably the best herbal liqueur in mixology, being compatible with almost everything. The only downside is that some people are especially sensitive to some of the component flavors and don't like it, while some older people find it just shouts Christmas very loudly due to the long history of it having been a holiday favorite. Never the less, the complexity and gingerbread notes of Benedictine can add amazing complexity to cocktails, as well as serving as a liaison between ingredients that wouldn't always get along, because it hits all of the ADSR envelope notes loud and clear (see page 66). While the exact recipe is only known by three people at a time, the known ingredients include angelica, hyssop, juniper, myrrh, saffron, mace, pine cones, aloe, arnica, lemon balm, tea leaves, thyme, coriander, cloves, lemon, vanilla beans, orange peel, honey, berries, cinnamon and nutmeg.

Jägermeister (35% Alcohol, 13% Sugar)

A German product first sold in the 1930's. They began an aggressive marketing campaign in the 1990's that dramatically increased sales, but somewhat damaged their reputation at the same time. Made with 56 botanical ingredients, the flavor is a bit medicinal with notes of cola, coffee, cherry, black pepper, cinnamon and mint. It can be used as an amaro to add complexity, but due to the marketing of it as an ice cold shot, it now has some negative sentiments among mixologists, because any cocktail that lists Jägermeister as an ingredient on a bar menu is often perceived as something for young people who just want to get drunk.

Chartreuse (Green: 55% Alcohol, 22% Sugar)

A French product. There is also a Yellow Chartreuse with a lower 43% alcohol content. Both are made from 130 different botanical ingredients in a secret formula going back centuries. Chartreuse easily dominates most cocktails due to its strong and unique flavor. It is a challenge to integrate it, but not impossible (*e.g. Pale Rainbow* on page 163). Green Chartreuse has a much sharper attack than Yellow in the ADSR envelope (see page 66), and has a strong lingering mint aftertaste that can potentially be reminiscent of mouthwash, depending on other ingredients in the cocktail. In addition to Green and Yellow, there are some less common varieties, such as MOF (45% alcohol) that is somewhere between the two common varieties. There are also quite a few versions that have been discontinued over the years and are highly collectible, sometimes selling for thousands at auction.

Drambuie (40% Alcohol, 34% Sugar)

Produced in Scotland. Very unusual for having a base of Scotch whisky from the Isle of Skye. The herbal flavor in this is second only to Benedictine in my opinion. Because it has a Scotch base, it is more restricted in what it can be paired with, but very worthwhile to explore.

Vana Tallinn (40 to 50% Alcohol, 32% Sugar)

This liqueur from Estonia is something every mixologist should get to know. The flavors are predominately vanilla, gingerbread and orange peel, but there is more going on. Vana Tallinn is produced in three versions, being 40, 45 and 50% alcohol. The 50% version is scarce outside of Estonia, but it is the best. Vana Tallinn truly deserves much more international fame.

Crème de Menthe (Bols & DeKuyper: 24% Alcohol, 36% Sugar)

Mint belongs to this category because it is an herb. Crème de Menthe comes in both white (clear) and green types. The latter is artificially colored. This is one of the only herbal liqueurs where the recipe is actually known because it is made in the same way as fruit liqueurs; It is simply mint macerated in neutral grain alcohol with water and sugar added. Tempus Fugit's white Crème de Menthe is better in flavor with 28% alcohol and less sugar (the exact amount of sugar is not known).

Valhalla (35% Alcohol, 15% Sugar)

Made in Finland. The principle herbal ingredients are actually stated and shown in pictures on the back label. Namely, angelica, wormwood and yarrow. The wormwood used is the same type in absinthe, but the flavor is not anise at all. It is unique and has the rare character of being able to be mixed with Scotch whisky.

Galliano L'Autentico (42.3% Alcohol, 25% Sugar)

This is a very unusual case among liqueurs. Back in the 1970's, they began changing the formula of Galliano and reducing the amount of alcohol. The flavor became very vanilla forward, and the alcohol dropped down to 30%. In 2006, the company changed the name of this new product to Galliano Vanilla (page 42) and re-introduced this original formula back on the market as Galliano L'Autentico. If you are making any older cocktail recipe that calls for Galliano, this is the one you need to use. However, if the recipe dates from the 1980's to 2005, "Galliano" refers to Galliano Vanilla in the current labeling.

Licor 43 / Licor Cuarenta y Tres (31% Alcohol, 39% Sugar)

This Spanish liqueur is made from 43 herbs and spices, but the dominant flavor is vanilla. More subtle notes include tea, coriander and cocoa. It is often added to coffee in Spain in the place of sugar, just as Sambuca is sometimes used for coffee in Italy.

Strega Liquore (40% Alcohol, 33% Sugar)

Produced in Italy for over 150 years. Strega is quite unusual among liqueurs for being aged in wood. Also because the botanicals and spices used are not local, but imported from many distant places. The flavor is sweet with notes of mint, lemon peel, licorice root, pine, vanilla and flowers. This is a great ingredient in mixology, and one that's often overlooked.

Becherovka (38% Alcohol, 10% Sugar)

From the Czech Republic. The flavor is cloves, apples, ginger, mint and "more than twenty" botanicals. The slight sweetness seems to come from honey rather than sugar, but the recipe is a secret. It has been compared to being like a version of a highly concentrated Falernum, and in fact it is an excellent addition to Falernum in a small amount. Becherovka is traditionally mixed with tonic water as a digestive.

Unicum Zwack (40% Alcohol, 17% Sugar)

This is the most famous Hungarian bitter liqueur, dating back to 1790. Like Jägermeister, it can play the role of an amaro. Zwack is another closely guarded recipe and considered an item of cultural heritage in Hungary. The flavor is very complex with notes of fennel, anise, jasmine, black pepper, coffee and root beer. It pairs especially well with Columbian rums.

Aquavit (O.P. Anderson: 40% Alcohol, 6% Sugar)

This traditional Scandinavian liqueur is distilled with caraway and dill seeds. Note that the word for caraway and the word for cumin are the same in much of Scandinavia and Eastern Europe, so there is frequent confusion of these two different spices. Many Aquavit manufacturers incorrectly state that cumin is the flavor when it is written in English. It is *always* caraway, in fact. There are different traditions of how and when to drink Aquavit that vary between Norway, Sweden, Finland, Iceland and Denmark. The two most common ways are ice cold as a shot, or at room temperature followed by a sip of beer. It is especially popular to drink with crayfish, which is a very popular traditional event in Finland every August.

Flaggpunsch (Carlshamns: 26% Alcohol, 27% Sugar)

A Swedish liquor that is consumed to some extent throughout all of Scandinavia. It is quite sweet with notes of dried pineapple and spices. Used in some cocktail recipes in Scandinavia, but seldom seen elsewhere.

Kümmel (40% Alcohol)

This German cumin and caraway liqueur was created by Helbing back in 1836. It was at the height of its popularity between 1940 and 1960, but now is largely forgotten. It is an ingredient in many cocktails from that period. Kümmel is related to Aquavit (see previous entry) but can contain as much as 35% sugar). It was originally a flavored brandy, but now is often made with neutral grain alcohol. Closely related is **Allasch**, produced in Latvia. Allasch is flavored with caraway, but also has citrus peel, almonds, and some botanicals usually seen in gin (but it does not have juniper).

Anise Family

Absinthe (Pernod brand: 68% Alcohol, 0% Sugar)

Nicknamed "The Green Fairy" because it was believed to cause such hallucinations, It was banned for decades as a supposedly dangerous narcotic due to an incorrect chemical analysis in the 19th century when such technology was still primitive. That mistake was eventually realized, but the reputation of Absinthe was already firmly established in the minds of most people. It is a very high alcohol content with an intense anise flavor and bitterness from the most potent type of wormwood. While that wormwood does contain a compound that causes hallucinations (thujone), but to consume enough of it by drinking Absinthe, you would be dead many times over from the alcohol content. Most of the time when Absinthe is used in a cocktail, it is in dropwise amounts or by rinsing the glass with a little (*e.g.* the Sazerac). There are many brands now, but Pernod's is still the best.

Pernod (40% Alcohol, 2.5% Sugar)

Originally produced as a replacement for Absinthe by the same company after Absinthe was banned (see Absinthe above). It is sweeter and not as intense as Absinthe *recette originale* (original recipe). After decades of this substitute having been manufactured and enjoyed by the public, Pernod has kept it on the market, even though they no longer legally need to.

Herbsaint (50% Alcohol)

This is an American product that was also produced as a substitute for Absinthe after it was banned. It is very much like Pernod, but with a higher alcohol concentration (but not as high as Absinthe). It has been appearing in cocktail recipes lately, but you can substitute Pernod without fear.

Pastis (Ricard: 40% Alcohol, 1% Sugar)

Yet another replacement for Absinthe that became very popular. This French product arrived later and from another company, but Ricard's formula is now produced by Pernod. It is so powerful in flavor that it is almost never seen in cocktail recipes. The taste is strongly anise with only faint notes of fennel, mint and lemon. Pastis should not be substituted for Absinthe or Pernod in a cocktail.

Anisette (25% Alcohol, approximately 20% Sugar)

This is the liqueur that made Marie Brizard famous, and it was their first product ever. Marie Brizard began producing this in 1755, which is decades before Absinthe was first produced, raising the question of whether Absinthe was inspired by this product. At any rate, Anisette stands as the most cocktail-friendly member of the anise group of spirits. It will not overpower a drink nearly as easily as Absinthe or Pernod, and it has less bitterness.

Ouzo (37.5 to 50% Alcohol, 20% Sugar)

This Greek liquor is not commonly seen in cocktails, and it is another example of something that deserves more attention by mixologists. The primary flavor is anise, but Ouzo also contains fennel, cardamom and other spices in small amounts. The origin of the name is disputed, but the best theory is that long ago the best quality Ouzo was being exported to France back when Ouzo was still called *Tsipouro*. The crates were labeled for shipping with the word "uso" followed by the destination, meaning *ship to*. This eventually became synonymous with meaning the best quality. Like many anise liquors, it turns milky when combined with water. This has been termed "the ouzo effect", because Ouzo is older than Absinthe.

Sambuca (38% Alcohol, 35-40% Sugar)

This is essentially a sweeter Italian version of Ouzo. Aside from anise, other ingredients are generally elderflower and licorice root. In Italy It Is common practice to put coffee beans in a shot of Sambuca. Sometimes the shot is ignited briefly to heat it. Because it is so sweet, sometimes it is used in place of sugar in coffee. Marie Brizard Anisette is preferred in cocktails.

Arak or Raki (50% or more Alcohol)

This is a strong Arabic version of Ouzo made from fermented grapes and star anise. Arak should not be confused with Arrack, which is a seldom seen Indonesian spirit made from fermented coconuts with no relation to Arak. Arak is almost never called for in cocktails, but it has potential.

FRUIT LIQUEURS

Most cocktails have some kind of fruit component. Liqueurs are all sweet by definition. There are literally hundreds of products in this category. Some of the most common include:

Cointreau (40% Alcohol, 23% Sugar)

This is the original quality orange liqueur. **Triple Sec** was developed as an inexpensive alternative for bars. Any recipe that calls for Triple Sec, can substitute Cointreau with superior results. In the 2010's **Cointreau Noir** and **Cointreau Blood Orange** were introduced, which are sweeter and intended for sipping straight. They are not a substitute, or even very useful.

Grand Marnier Cordon Rouge (40% Alcohol, 20% Sugar)

Cordon Rouge means red ribbon, and it's the Grand Marnier one normally sees. While most liqueurs are based on neutral grain spirits, Grand Marnier is based on cognac. It is an intense, rich orange liqueur with strong notes of cognac. There are some special editions, such as the formula celebrating their 150th anniversary, *Cuvée du Cent Cinquantenaire*, containing cognac aged for up to 50 years (and priced accordingly). Those are intended for consuming straight and do not work as well in cocktails as one might hope, because they are sweeter and softer on the palate.

Pierre Ferrand Dry Curaçao (40% Alcohol, 18% Sugar)

This orange liqueur is especially notable for having very low sugar as liqueurs go. This is especially valuable because more can be used without making a cocktail cloyingly sweet.

Merlet Trois Citrus (40% Alcohol, 15% Sugar)

Although it also says Triple Sec on the label in small print, this is just to establish the category of liqueur it is, and should not be taken as an indication of inferior quality in the way Tripe Sec is usually regarded. Merlet Trois Citrus is made by macerating orange, grapefruit and lemon peels in neutral grain alcohol. Like Pierre Ferrand Dry Curaçao (see above) it is very low in sugar as citrus liqueurs go. It offers more complexity than Pierre Ferrand's product, but not as much specific orange flavor.

Parfait Amour (Bols: 24% Alcohol, 30% Sugar)

This was often used in place of Crème de Violette, as it was easier to find and is also flavored with violets (among other things). More subtle notes include orange peel, roses, vanilla and almonds. It is tricky to use in complex cocktails, often tasting like scented bath soap if you aren't careful.

Blue Curaçao (Bols: 21% Alcohol, 25% Sugar
DeKuyper: 20% Alcohol, 31% Sugar)

This is just Triple Sec with blue food coloring added. It is inferior to Cointreau in flavor and is only useful for its blue color. Decades ago, Bols also made a **Green Curaçao**. The alcohol for both was originally 35%. The quality was reasonably decent back then. Now it is truly miserable.

Mandarine Napoleon (38% Alcohol, 26% Sugar)

Aside from the namesake ingredient of mandarine oranges, there are 20 other botanical ingredients, some of which are green tea, coriander and cumin. It is also blended with cognac and aged for 3 years before being bottled. Therefore it is not merely a mandarine orange version of Cointreau.

Mandarino, Don Giovanni (32% Alcohol, 28% Sugar)

This is a complex Italian mandarine orange based liqueur from locally grown seasonal fruit. On its own, it has a bit of a synthetic aftertaste, but this doesn't come through when mixed in a cocktail. It is rather different from Mandarine Napoleon with other peculiar herbal notes that defy description.

Limoncello (Isolabella: 30% Alcohol, 26% Sugar)

The liqueur of Sicily and southern Italy. This has a sweet natural lemon flavor, being made from the zest of a special variety native to the region, called Femminello St. Teresa lemons. Any time there is lemon juice and sugar called for in a recipe, Limoncello is a candidate to experiment with.

Maraschino Liqueur (Luxardo: 32% Alcohol, 37% Sugar)

There are several brands, the most well known good one being Luxardo. However, much better is Maraska from Croatia. Most other brands range from quite bad to absolutely terrible. Stick to Luxardo or Maraska.

Heering Cherry Liqueur (24% Alcohol, 31% Sugar)

This Danish liqueur has been produced for more than 200 years. While there are many other cherry liqueurs on the market, Heering is the best for having a pure cherry taste that is not synthetic, unlike many other brands.

Cherry Brandy (Bols: 24% Alcohol)

There are many brands labeled as Cherry Brandy, many of which do not contain any brandy. Bols' product is made from cherries and cherry pits, but it is not as rich as Heering or some other luxury liqueurs like Giffard's. Both Bols' and other quality products have a slight almond flavor, unlike Heering.

Guignolet de Dijon (18% Alcohol)

Produced by Gabriel Boudier, this is made from four types of black cherries. The taste is almost pure black cherry juice with just a little sugar.

Peach Liqueur (16.5% Alcohol, 29% Sugar)

The original product by DeKuyper is Peachtree Liqueur (sometimes called Peachtree Schnapps). It has the flavor of both ripe and slightly unripe green peaches. The flavor arrives quickly on the palate. Giffard's *Péche de Vigne* has only the flavor of ripe peaches and arrives on the palate slightly later and with some pleasant perfume notes in the Decay of the ADSR envelope (see page 66). Giffard's product is made from a special type of peach grown in Lyon, France, that have a slightly different flavor.

Crème de Cassis (Merlet: 20% Alcohol, 57% Sugar)

This is a very sweet blackcurrant liqueur that is most often seen in the well known Kir Royale cocktail, being combined with champagne. The alcohol and sugar content vary with brand, but only by a little.

Crème de Mûre (Giffard: 16% Alcohol)

This is blackberry liqueur. The name is in French. It is slightly different from Crème de Cassis, as you would expect from a different fruit. Seldom called for in cocktail recipes these days, but quite popular long ago.

Chambord Liqueur (16.5% Alcohol, 29% Sugar)

This is a black raspberry liqueur that is vaguely similar to both Crème de Cassis and Crème de Mure (see previous two entries). Raspberry syrup mixed with vodka in the ratio of 3:1, is sometimes substituted in a pinch.

Amaretto DiSaronno (28% Alcohol, 31% Sugar)

This Italian almond and fruit liqueur is used in countless cocktails. There are many amarettos made by other companies, but DiSaronno is the best. It differs from Orgeat Syrup in having more of a sharp almond extract taste due to distillation, and of course having alcohol in it. Another almond flavoring for cocktails is Nardini alla Mandorla Grappa (see page 40).

Coconut Liqueur (Marie Brizard: 20% Alcohol)

The essence of pure coconut in a clear (not cloudy) sweet liqueur. A much better alternative to the canned coconut cream usually used in recipes. This is a product that works especially well in tropical drinks, but it is usually quite hard to find.

Coconut Rum (Malibu: 21% Alcohol, 21% Sugar)

Often ridiculed by cocktail enthusiasts as being synthetic tasting and not really either rum or a coconut liqueur. The main advantage is that it's readily available in stores. In a bar, most customers either won't notice the difference or don't care. However, if you are a perfectionist, then there is a recipe for a far superior coconut rum you can make yourself on page 198.

Crème de Banana (Bols: 17% Alcohol, 30% Sugar)

Almost any recipe that calls for this is referring to the Bols or DeKuyper product. A far superior Crème de Banana for richness is the Tempus Fugit liqueur, which has a different deep roasted banana flavor. Any time this is specified in a recipe, you can substitute the product you can make yourself using the recipe on page 180. Many prefer this even to Tempus Fugit's.

Pisang Ambon (Bols: 17% Alcohol, 19% Sugar
DeKuyper: 15% Alcohol, 36% Sugar)

This is from unripe green bananas. The Cavendish cultivar banana is the one most familiar to people. That's the banana used to produce most other banana liqueurs. Pisang is made from the Gros Michel cultivar, which actually used to be the most commonly exported banana until a plague of a banana disease wiped out much of the crops back in the 1950's. Cavendish proved to be resistant to the disease, and so they became the bananas we have in grocery stores today. The two main suppliers of Pisang are Bols and DeKuyper. It is worth noting that DeKuyper's contains nearly twice as much sugar, and also that Bols' is not in the usual Bols style bottle, but rather masquerading as an import from Indonesia.

Midori Melon Liqueur (20% Alcohol, 28% Sugar)

Originally from Japan, this bright green melon liqueur is now made in several different countries to meet the demand. Because it has a strong and unique flavor, it is difficult to use without it being the star of the show, so it mixes best with vodka or light rum. Many love it, but some truly hate it.

Fruit Brandy Family

These are distilled spirits with very little to no sugar added. They are not commonly seen in cocktails, but are quite useful.

Calvados and Applejack (Apple)

Since these can be used as base spirits in cocktails, they have been listed in a later section of this book (see page 55).

Kirschwasser or Kirsch (Schladerer: 42% Alcohol)

Mostly manufactured in Germany from Morello cherries in the Black Forest (Schwarzwälder) region. It has no discernable sugar, and so is very different from cherry liqueur or cherry brandy. This is another underused ingredient by most mixologists. It offers funky, grassy cherry notes in the finish (the Release phase of the ADSR envelope—see page 66) that can harmonize with many other flavors for complexity and an extended finish.

Mirabelle and Slivovitz

There are two principle varieties of this. One is sweetened as a liqueur, such as that made in France from a type of small yellow plums. A sweetened version also exists in Poland, but is seldom seen elsewhere. There is an unsweetened version that is made from damson plums that is usually called Slivovitz across many parts of Europe including Bulgaria, Croatia, Hungary, and more. Some are aged for years in barrels, adding complexity and color. These are rarely seen in cocktail recipes, but they offer interesting novel flavors for the intrepid mixologist.

Grappa or Marc

This grape brandy is rarely a flavoring, but occasionally used as a base spirit in cocktails, so it has been mentioned in that section on page 58.

Nardini alla Mandorla Grappa (50% Alcohol, 2% Sugar)

An Italian product. Although this is based on grappa, it has almost none of the usual grassy notes in grappa. It is more like Amaretto but with almost no sugar and some subtle cherry notes, because the ingredients are almonds and maraschino cherries. In cocktail design, this occupies a unique place in mixology and should be implemented much more. However, it can be very difficult to obtain, depending on what country you are in.

Apricot Brandy/Liqueur (Bols: 24% Alcohol, 25% Sugar
DeKuyper: 20% Alcohol, 32% Sugar)

This is the most confusing of the fruit brandies. There are many types and names:

> Abricot Eau de Vie (France)
>
> Marillenschnaps (Austria and Germany)
>
> Pálinka (Czech Republic)
>
> Meruňkovice (Hungary)
>
> Kaïsiya Rakia (Bulgaria)

It is especially important to know that "apricot brandy" may contain neither brandy or apricots! The term "apricot brandy" has been used to mean apricot liqueur for a very long time, but a similar flavor can be obtained from distilling certain cherries in plain alcohol. This is also used to produce some Cherry Brandy. With that in mind, the Croatian company Maraska, which produces the finest Maraschino liqueur in the world, also produces an Apricot Brandy that is simply awful. At least they label it as "imitation". Some other manufacturers are not so honest. Regulations about what is allowed to be called Apricot Brandy vary between nations with no international standard at all. To make matters even more difficult to sort out, some companies have drastically changed their formula over the years.

For a _true_ Apricot Liqueur, the best are made by Merlet and Giffard. The two most common brands are Bols and DeKuyper, though:

Bols Apricot Brandy is produced from apricot kernels distilled with alcohol. Then it is mixed with apricot juice and some brandy. Bols admits their formula has changed a lot over time. Undoubtedly this was to keep the cost of production down to make a more affordable product. Decades ago, Bols Apricot Brandy was more similar to Giffard's product today. So if you are following a recipe from before about 1965, it more like expects a liqueur such as Merlet's product, even if Bols brand is explicitly called for.

DeKuyper Apricot Brandy is produced as an infusion of brandy with apricots and sugar in a way similar to the recipe in this book on page 202. The alcohol content used to be 24% but is now 20%, and other changes to the formula have likely happened over the years, too. Consider that the type of brandy used is logically quite poor in order for the finished product to sell for so little even after the addition of apricots! While it is an acceptable product in average cocktails, it is not as intense or rich as Merlet's product. For a _true_ Apricot Liqueur, the best choice is Merlet followed by Giffard.

THERE ARE STILL MANY MORE

There are countless other seldom-seen fruit liqueurs including ones from figs, quince, lychees and more, as well as proprietary blends of fruits with other fruits, herbs, nuts and spices. Nearly all of these have applications in cocktails, but most are hard to come by and many are so obscure that publishing a recipe that is based on them is pointless because almost no one will be able to acquire the specified ingredient(s).

This, once again, is why I have provided recipes in this book to enable anyone to produce key flavor ingredients for themselves with ordinary supermarket foods and a few things that can easily be acquired online (specifically citrus oils and a fine mesh sieve).

OTHER COMPONENTS

These are ingredients that do not fit neatly into any other category.

Ginger Liqueur (Bols: 24% Alcohol, 25% Sugar)

Your basic ginger liqueur. It is sweet and gingery without bringing any other real notes in. The ginger hit is fast on the palate, so it has its place in cocktail design, but there are certainly more sophisticated choices. This is the Triple Sec of ginger liqueurs.

Ginger of the Indies (35% Alcohol)

This is Giffard's take on ginger liqueurs, and it is far superior to Bols with additional complexity of coriander seeds, green cardamom and oranges. It still has plenty of spicy ginger, though it arrives later on the palate than in the Bols' product, which is especially useful in layering flavors.

Ratzingwer Ingwerlikör (35% Alcohol, 14% Sugar)

This German ginger liqueur made with neutral grain alcohol is more complex with notes of orange peel, vanilla and some faint spices. Although rarely seen in cocktail recipes, this is another example of an ingredient that *should* be used more by mixologists looking for unique flavors that can be poured straight out of a bottle.

Domain de Canton Ginger Liqueur (28% Alcohol)

This is a French cognac-based ginger liqueur. The complexity comes from the cognac, which may or may not be useful in cocktail construction depending on what else you are mixing it with. You can think of it as the ginger version of Grand Marnier (which is a cognac version of Cointreau).

Frangelico (20% Alcohol, 23% Sugar)

This hazelnut liqueur has changed its formula over the years, now with lower alcohol and less of the sharp attack it once had, unfortunately. It is now more like a mixture of vodka and hazelnut syrup, but still worthwhile.

Galliano Vanilla (30% Alcohol, 25% Sugar)

For many years between the 1970's and 2005, this was simply called Galliano because the company had changed the formula. In 2006, they re-introduced the original Galliano and named the one it had mutated into as Galliano Vanilla. For more on this, see Galliano L'Autentico on page 32.

As the name suggests, this is like a combination of the mildly anise flavored Galliano infused with vanilla. But it is not quite that simple. It is arguably just as useful in cocktails as the traditional Galliana L'Autentico.

Butterscotch Liqueur (Bols: 24% Alcohol, 43% Sugar)

Although this has a slightly synthetic taste straight out of the bottle, in small amounts in a cocktail, it can add a mysterious and complex sweetness because the taste is so rarely encountered. Balance is the key.

Sour Rhubarb Liqueur (DeKuyper: 15% Alcohol, 28% Sugar)

This is an interesting component to use in mixology because of the long delay before the complex tastes emerge on the palate. At first all you taste is sugar, but after several seconds there is more. Unfortunately, this product can be hard to find. Rhubarb is a common ingredient in amari, so it can be used to exaggerate those notes in a cocktail with the right amaro.

Elixir de Cuba

This is a curiious product that defies easy categorization. It is banned in the United States due to their long standing Cuban embargo, but it is widely available everywhere else. It is a blend of aged Cuban rums that are used to macerate raisins in a commercial process that is very much like the homemade rum modifications that I detailed in my *Cocktails of the South Pacific* book. The sugar content is much higher than ordinary rums, but not so much as a liqueur. Some dislike it as being too sweet, but it is very popular in Spain and the Czech Republic for an apertif straight out of the bottle over ice. It can add sweetness and complexity to rum cocktails, but it does have some other notes that do not harmonize with everything due to the raisins. This is a fantastic ingredient when used judiciously.

Falernum

For many bartenders and cocktail enthusiasts, Falernum is synonymous with the product made by John D. Taylor, called "Velvet Falernum" (11% alcohol). It is perfectly clear (not cloudy or translucent as many falernum syrups are), however it lacks flavor and is quite sweet. It can be thought of as a gently flavored Barbados rum syrup for the most part. The main advantage is that it is clear, which is aesthetically important in cocktails served straight up. Other Falernums are usually more intense, but cloudy. See the Falernum recipe in this book on page 177.

Fassionola

This was the creation of Donn Beach back in the 1930's and is used almost exclusively for Tiki style drinks, and in particular, the Cobra Fang and Hurricane. The main flavors are passonfruit. berries, pineapple, and hibiscus. The recipe for my version is on page 192. Sometimes it is sold as a non-alcoholic syrup. Although this is normally used in tropical drinks, it harmonizes very well with the Italian Amaro *Montenegro*, and it can be used with base spirits other than rum. Especially vodka and brandy.

Stroh

Made in Austria since the 1850's, it comes in many different strengths ranging from 38 to 80% alcohol. Note that in the United States, Stroh is labeled in proof rather than ABV, so Stroh 80 = Stroh 160 in the U.S. This is a spiced rum technically, but it has little in common with any other rum — and that's saying a lot considering how diverse rums are. The flavor is butterscotch and gasoline. It seems to be consumed in Austria mostly for the sole purpose of getting drunk. Never the less, in small amounts it can actually be used in cocktails with the same care one would exercise with nitroglycerine. Do not substitute Stroh 80/160 for a 151-proof rum. Never.

Zirbenz

Made in Austria. Also called the "Stone Pine Liqueur of the Alps." It is flavored with blue pine cones that only grow high in the Swiss Alps. The flavor has only faint pine notes compared to Finnish and Russian pine liqueurs (which are more reminiscent of floor polish to the uninitiated). Zirbenz is another example of a product that has a lot of potential in mixology, but has not yet been realized. It is somewhat difficult to find, but well worth seeking out if you are looking to capitalize on novel flavors that your patrons are unlikely to have ever heard of.

Coffee Family

Lua Licor de Café (30% Alcohol)

This is the finest coffee liqueur that I know of. Unlike most coffee liqueurs that are an infusion of ordinarly grain alcohol, Lua's alcohol is distilled from fermented regional grapes from Spain and it is flavored with the famous Jamaican Blue Mountain coffee beans, deeply roasted. There are notes of spice, wood, dark chocolate, charcoal and very faint cigar smoke.

Mr. Black Cold Brew Coffee Liqueur (23% Alcohol)

One of the newer products on the market, this Australian coffee liqueur is less sweet than most and slightly bitter. There are faint notes of vanilla, orange and dark chocolate. Not as complex or rich as Lua, but good in its own way. It is not a direct substitute for other coffee liqueurs, be advised.

Kahlúa (20% Alcohol except 21.5% in Ohio, 39% Sugar)

This Mexican product is mostly flavored with Arabica coffee, but there is some vanilla and caramel added. It is sweet to the point of being somewhat syrupy, but the pleasant afternotes of vanilla and white chocolate have made it the best selling coffee liqueur in the world since the 1960's.

Kahlúa Especial (36% Alcohol)

This premium grade Kahlúa has less sugar and is less viscous. The flavor is more intense, which means it is a superior product, but also means that it is not a direct substitution for any recipe calling for Kahlúa. This is only available in some markets as of the time of this writing, mostly in duty free shops in airports and for some unknown reason, Ohio state liquor stores.

Tia Maria (20% Alcohol, 31% Sugar)

From Italy. The flavor is similar to Kahlúa, but lighter and not quite as sweet. It is flavored with Arabica coffee, vanilla beans, spices and blended with some Jamaican overproof white rum (the amount of each is a secret).

Galliano Ristretto (30% Alcohol, 38% Sugar)

Like Galliano Vanilla, this is more than just original Galliano with some coffee added. It is its own thing. As such it is not useful as a direct substitute for a coffee liqueur in any cocktail.

Chocolate Family

Crème de Cacao (White) (Bols: 24% Alcohol, 30% Sugar)

Clear colored chocolate liqueur. Not white chocolate. Bols' products usually have less sugar than DeKuyper's, as is the case here.

Crème de Cacao (Dark) (DeKuyper: 20% Alcohol, 42% Sugar)

Dark colored chocolate liqueur. Tempus Fugit produces a richer version with vanilla included at 24% alcohol, but is more than twice as expensive.

Mozart Black (17% Alcohol)

This is 87% cocoa according to the manufacturer, making it the most bittersweet chocolate liqueur on the market. There are many flavors of Mozart chocolate liqueurs that could be used in place of Crème de Cacao in a recipe to personalize it, but Mozart *Black* stands out as being very dark and much more intense.

Godiva Dark Chocolate Liqueur (15% Alcohol)

From the Belgian chocolate company, this is a rich version of dark Crème de Cacao, but not as intense as Mozart Black. Also in **White Chocolate**.

Sabra (30% Alcohol)

This is a chocolate and orange liqueur from Israel. There are also some faint botanical notes. Unfortunately, this is also difficult to obtain in much of the world. An acceptable substitute for cocktails can be prepared by mixing Dark Crème de Cacao, Cointreau and Grand Marnier in the ratio of 8:2:1.

Cream Liqueur Family

These are liqueurs that contain milk or cream. According to most manufacturers, the shelf life on them is two years without being opened and six months after opening if they are stored in the refrigerator. Opened without refrigeration they spoil within days.

Bailey's Irish Cream (17% Alcohol, 20% Sugar)

Introduced in 1974, this became an instant classic with, shall we say, a less discriminating crowd. It contains cream, Irish whiskey and cocoa flavor. There are several classic shots and cocktails based on Bailey's, of course, but this liqueur is hard to keep in the background of anything complex.

Kyrö Dairy Cream (16% Alcohol, 20% Sugar)

Produced in Finland by the same distillary that has won first place international awards for its gin, so you might expect this to be gin based. It is not. It has rye whiskey, toffee, cinnamon and a hint of licorice. It is a more sophisticated version of Bailey's, to put it succinctly. It is difficult to obtain outside of Finland, but there is a recipe for simulating it on page 201.

Yogurt Liqueur (15% Alcohol, 20% Sugar)

Produced mainly by Bols. It is very much like yogurt, sugar and vodka shaken up together. In fact, that's probably exactly what it is. Rarely seen as a cocktail ingredient because yogurt tends to clash with everything.

Advocaat (15% Alcohol, 26% Sugar)

This is a Dutch invention of cream, eggs, honey, vanilla and brandy. It is very much reminiscent of Christmas Egg Nog if it was made in a distillery. Much like the Yogurt Liqueur above, it has a hard time working in a cocktail recipe because you end up with an Egg Nog variant or something weird.

Spice Family

Although countless liquors and liqueurs have spices as flavorings, this section refers to those that are based on a particular spice or that are spicy hot from chilies.

Cinnamon Schnapps

This is the generic name for many liqueurs flavored with cinnamon. The term "schnapps" is German for any strong liquor. Because cinnamon and peppermint have been popular in Germany for centuries, the name schnapps has been carried on by many manufacturers for those two flavors.

Gold Strike (50% Alcohol, 20% Sugar)

This is a high-alcohol cinnamon schnapps with flakes of real gold in it. The flakes are so small and thin that they are worth only pennies.

Goldschläger (40% Alcohol)

This is just another brand of cinnamon schnapps, but with a slightly lower alcohol content. It has the same gold flake gimmick.

Fireball (33% Alcohol, 23% Sugar)

This is a cinnamon liqueur based on rye whiskey. Mildly spicy, less alcohol and no gold flakes. This is a very useful ingredient in small amounts.

Pimento or Allspice Dram (Bitter Truth: 22.5% Alcohol)

This is essentially rum flavored with allspice berries and sugar or caramel. It was originally produced in Jamaica. It is almost exclusively used in rum cocktails, and especially Tiki style drinks. St. Elizabeth Allspice Dram from Austria is another excellent brand of the same thing.

Ancho Reyes Ancho Chile Liqueur (40% Alcohol, 13% Sugar)

Made in Mexico. Ancho is the name given to dried Poblano chilies. This one comes in a brown bottle. See the next item below for the other one. The flavor is chili heat with subtle notes of cocoa and cinnamon. It plays best with tequila and mezcal, but with sufficient imagination, you can make it work with brandy and vodka, too.

Ancho Reyes Poblano Liqueur (40% Alcohol, 15% Sugar)

Also called Ancho Reyes *Verde*. When you are behind the bar, this is best remembered as "the one in the green bottle". Made from fresh Poblano chilies, the flavor difference from the Ancho Chile liqueur (listed immediately above) is exactly the same as the difference between Ancho and Poblano chilies, as you would expect. This is also quite spicy and suited primarily to tequila and mezcal cocktails, but not exclusively. Also, I have duplicated their incorrect spelling of Chile here, which refers to the nation of Chile and not chili peppers. This is a common spelling mistake, but rather surprising to see on a manufactured product. It has nothing to do with Chile.

Absolut Peppar (40% Alcohol, 0% Sugar)

Infusing vodka with chili peppers is ancient. It is a popular, though very pedestrian Nastoyka in Russia. There is little flavor other than heat, so it is of limited use. Ancho Reyes' products (see above) are superior overall due to their layers of flavor.

THE BIG GUNS

Now the base liquors of cocktails need to be addressed...

VODKA and FLAVORED VODKAS

Unflavored vodka is a neutral spirit by design. In a cocktail with any strong flavors, it makes very little difference which brand you use. Just avoid anything <u>so</u> inexpensive that it has a foul aroma or odd taste, obviously.

Flavored vodkas are another matter, but in most cases, they should be avoided. Instead, use plain vodka and add your own flavorings. There are a few exceptions such as Absolut Extrakt, which is distilled with cardamom and other botanicals that make it more like a gin without the juniper. Also Absolut Pears, which has a strong natural pear flavor and no added sugar. Absolut Peppar, Finlandia Mango Vodka and Stolichnaya Salted Caramel Vodka are also worthwhile. Just about everything else in this category is not.

GIN and GENEVER

The original gin was Dutch Genever (often spelled *Jenever*). Genever is the Dutch word for juniper. This is not a history book, but the reason juniper and other botanicals were added originally was to help mask some of the nasty taste in the poorly distilled alcohol they were making using crude ceramic alembic stills, because better equipment had yet to be invented. The juniper flavor became popular and eventually as distilling practices improved, gin as we know it today was reborn in London.

Genever is subdivided into old (*oude*) and young (*jonge*), but this is not about aging. Rather, it refers to the production method and some legal specifications. Genever was originally produced from malt wine, not grain alcohol the way that London Gin is made. During World War I, malt became difficult to get, so grain was used to help shore up the supply of alcohol. Soon after that, this new type of Genever caught on, being mostly made from grain alcohol. So the legal definitions now are that old (*oude*) must contain at least 15% malt wine and less than 2% sugar, while new (*jonge*) Genever must contain *less* than 15% malt wine and less than 1% sugar. Most agree that old (*oude*) Genever is of superior quality.

All other gins (not Genever) are flavored neutral grain spirits with the only unifying characteristic of having juniper as their major flavor. Today there are hundreds of different gins on the market ranging from those very mild in flavor such as Finsbury to extremely strong in flavor, such as Kyrö Napue. There are also some flavored gins, but the same that I wrote about flavored vodka goes for gins, in that you are generally much better off adding whatever flavoring agent you like to a quality plain gin. Products like strawberry gin are usually synthetic tasting. As with flavored vodkas, there are a few odd exceptions (*e.g.* Tanqueray Rangpur Gin because it is made with an exotic fruit that is rarely seen and has a great flavor).

London Dry Gin does not contain sugar, which makes it suited to mixing with dry vermouth that most other spirits clash with. The unusual Martini made with Genever uses sweet vermouth, not dry.

There is a general rule that gin cocktails should be stirred and not shaken. The reason is that high quality gins have some delicate aldehydes that flavor them. These are prone to autoxidation (the reaction with oxygen in the air) which changes their flavor for the worse. However, if you are using a lesser quality gin, there is not so much to worry about as long as you don't shake it too vigorously. Some gin cocktails do require vigorous shaking though, such as a Ramos Fizz, but then there is cream and egg in it, making it impossible to notice the *bruised gin*, as it is called.

The natural question that comes to mind on this topic is why **James Bond** requested his Martini shaken and not stirred? That's considered a bad move by any bartender. In interviews, the author

Ian Fleming, defended this by saying James Bond wanted a more dilute Martini so he wouldn't become drunk. However, this is a bogus explanation, because it still contains the same amount of alcohol. More likely, Fleming just didn't realize the not-so-cool move he had Bond making at the time, and didn't want to admit it.

In addition to London Dry Gin, there is **Old Tom Gin** which does have sugar added to it, and generally a different collection of botanical ingredients, though juniper is still the main flavor.

Then there is **Bathtub Gin**, which was invented during Prohibition as a way to make a gin substitute without distillation by flavoring moonshine or medicinal alcohol with juniper and herbs. The mixture was then filtered through a pillow case. The resulting product was usually quite crude, so sugar was added to help make it palatable. Nearly all bathtub gins were also Old Tom gins.

Finally there is **Sloe Gin**, which is made with sloes (the fruit of a plant similar to plums) macerated in grain alcohol, not gin. It is also sweetened. Even though this is still called "gin" for historical reasons, it generally contains no juniper and not much else other than sloes. The Sloe Gin produced in the United States is made with berries and is not a true Sloe Gin.

RUM and RHUM

Without question, rum is the most diverse of all the distilled spirits. There are so many methods and formulas that the word "rum" by itself is almost meaningless. But rum is basically just sugar that's been fermented and distilled, right? Well, *basically*. Choose one from each of the columns below...

STARTING MATERIAL	STILL TYPE	AGING
Pure Sugar + Yeast	Copper Pot Still	None
Pure Sugar + Wild Yeast	Double Pot Still	Virgin White Oak
Sugar + Molasses	Column Still	French Oak
Pure Molasses	Pot & Column Blend	Sherry Barrels
Molasses + "Dregs"	Kettle or Alembic Still	Other Used Barrels

Even without any of the other basic factors such as the number of years it was aged, already there are dozens of possibilities—and no international standard. Even the ultra-simplified categories of light rum, gold rum and dark rum are misleading because caramel is often added to white rums to make them darker, and some dark rums are filtered through charcoal to remove coloring!

The terms "dark" and "light" are now largely obsolete. The only real fork in the road is agricole rhums, which are fundamentally very different tasting.

Agricole rhum begins with raw sugar cane and not molasses. Because of this, agricole rhum has what are termed "grassy notes" from the plant matter that went in along with the sugar. It usually also has what is usually termed "funk", meaning something a bit foul that is an acquired taste. This is why reviews online of agricole rhums are often peppered with loathing comments from people who didn't know what they were getting.

Agricole rhums are made in many different nations using many different methods, but the most widely known Agricole rhum is from Martinique, a French colony (which is why it has the French spelling, *rhum)*. When you see Martinique Rhum, it is an agricole product because that's all they make there. The convention of spelling rum as *rhum* for an agricole rhum is now used elsewhere.

One-style-per-country is typical. For example, all rums from Guyana are demerara rums. This is named for the place in Guyana called Demerara, not to be confused with demerara sugar which is a light brown partially refined sugar that can come from any country in the world that produces sugarcane. Confused yet? It gets worse.

In addition to the length of time and the type of wood that a rum is aged in, many rums are aged in barrels that were previously used to age sherry, cognac, bourbon and even Scotch whisky. In Barbados (as well as some other places), rum is aged in different types of barrels and then blended together to taste. Consequently, Barbados rums are among the most complex of all rums and can be very deep in taste.

Not to diminish Jamaican rums, some of which are the most intense of all, such as Smith & Cross (a key element in many classic Tiki cocktails owing to its unique character). Jamaican rums are nearly always concentrated in flavor, but not usually complex.

Aside from the length of time a rum is aged, the temperature and humidity are also factors. Rums aged in tropical climates will be different from ones in cooler places, such as temperature controlled buildings or caves. One especially interesting case is rum produced in Italy from imported sugar and molasses. Because it is aged in a cooler nation, the rum is unique (see page 129).

The other thing worth keeping in mind is that sugarcane is subect to *terroir* in the same way that Old World wines are. That is, depending on the soil, the climate and the surrounding crops, the flavor of the rum will vary. This is incredibly pronounced in rums from Columbia that have strong coffee notes and rums from Madagascar with strong vanilla notes, because these regions are predominantly growing coffee and vanilla, respectively. The air is filled with those aromas as the sugarcane is growing.

There is no way to even begin to scratch the surface here on all of the differences in rums from the dozens of countries that produce them and how changes in production methods affected vintage bottles, or this book would be an encyclopedia. Suffice it to say that the diversity is nearly infinite, and a different rum in a cocktail can make as dramatic of a difference as the entire rest of the recipe.

The recipes in this book have *mostly* been tailored to fairly common rums, but in some instances the recipe will only shine if you employ the specified rum. There is no way around that because one rum to another can be as different as gin is to cognac, and swapping gin for cognac in a recipe is never going to produce the intended taste, right?

Nearly all rums have some sugar or caramel added to them. Bacardi and Captain Morgan rums are around 2% sugar, while most other rums are less than 1%. These numbers are deceptive though, since caramel is a sweetener that is not measured directly. The point is that since all rums contain some sweetener, this makes them the ideal choice for sweet and sour cocktails. Think of any well known rum drink, and it will nearly always contain some citrus to balance the sweetness.

The flavor profiles are so vastly different from rum to rum that there is no point in even attempting to make any blanket statement about either the flavors or the ADSR curve (see page 66).

CACHAÇA

This is an agricole rhum produced in Brazil. The name cachaça is legally protected under international law as indicating it was made in Brazil. Less than 1% of the cachaça made is exported, with the majority of that goes to Germany.

Cachaça is distilled in copper pot stills. The problem with that is years ago international standards set a maximum level of copper ions that could be contained in any food or liquor for international commerce, and *real* cachaça exceeds that limit. It's not really an issue unless you are drinking it regularly, but the law is the law. So all exported cachaça must undergo an intense filtration process to remove the copper. Unfortunately, this is quite detrimental to the flavor, so unless you travel to Brazil and get the local product, you are not really tasting what cachaça is. Personally, knowing what it is supposed to taste like from before the rules changed, I never use this new version. It shouldn't even be sold as cachaça in my opinion.

COGNAC and BRANDY

Brandy and cognac are both made from fermented grapes. Essentially being distilled wine. Grappa (also called Marc in some countries) is also made from grapes, but only the seeds, stems and leaves are used (called the pomace) and not the juice, so it is very different.

All Cognac is brandy that has been produced in the Cognac region of France under rules imposed there. This is similar to how the Champagne region of France is the only place that can legally produce champagne. Everywhere else in the world must call it sparkling wine, even if it is made in the exact same way. Similarly, brandy can be made anywhere in the world, but no matter how it is made, it can not legally be called Cognac unless it was produced in Cognac, France. Never the less, there is Moldavian and Armenian "cognac". Although there are some 200 brands of cognac in that region of France, nearly all exports come from just five distilleries, namely Remy-Martin, Martell, Courvoisier, Hennessy and Ferrand.

Cognacs are rated by age as *VS* (2 to 3 years), *VSOP* (4 to 9 years), *XO* (10 to 13 years), *XXO* (14 or more years) and Hors d'Age (30 years or more, sometimes over a century). There is also the designation *Napoleon Cognac*, which is aged 6 to 9 years. Technically Napoleon Cognacs are also *VSOP*, but Napolean specifies 6 years or more, while *VSOP* could be aged 4 to 5 years only. Most cocktails benefit from *VSOP* refinement, while *XO* is usually excessive.

Brandy uses the same system to denote its age, but outside of the Cognac region of France, it is not regulated and sometimes used only as a general guide to quality from that distillery. In many countries a star (✰) rating system is used, where 5 stars (✰✰✰✰✰) is equivalent to *VSOP*.

In Spain, brandy that comes from the Jerez region has it's own system to express age, since it is generally aged much less. Those designations are:

Brandy de Jerez Solera: 6 months old
Brandy de Jerez Solera Reserva: 1 year old
Brandy de Jerez Solera Gran Reserva: 3 years old

Some of this is used in the production of Sherry. Among Spanish brandies, Torres is arguably the best value. There are two designations for their main products: Torres 10 and Torres 20, with 10 being aged in the Solera system (see page 3) and Torres 20 being left in single barrels. None of their products states the age; only that they are "aged for several years." There is also Torres 10 *Double Barrel*, which is halfway to being a cognac, but only halfway.

When it comes to mixing drinks, cognac is much heavier and richer than brandy. To put it into words, cognac adds *weight* to a cocktail, while brandies contain much of the same flavor but are usually not as heavy. Individual flavors of cognacs vary, but my usual choice for cocktails is Hennessy *VSOP* (specified in most of the recipes in this book). The individual flavors for me In order are: Apricot, lemon, oak, cloves and alcohol. Note that tastes are different for different people and change as you get older. Also note that when it is mixed with other ingredients, this sequence will change for technical biological reasons (taste receptors being temporarily blocked or amplified). There is no way to accurately predict this. You have to make your own charts (pages 68-69).

ARMAGNAC

In some ways, what Cognac is to Brandy, Armagnac is to Cognac in terms of floral notes and complexity. One main difference is that cognacs are distilled twice using a pot still, while armagnac is distilled once in a column still—but a short column still, which is rather unusual in liquor production. Brandy and Cognac are not really drinkable until they have been aged in wood, while Armagnac is drinkable even before it is aged because it has more flavor and fruitiness in it. The real difference comes from the extreme length of time that quality Armagnac is often aged. It is an uncommon cocktail ingredient. When it does show up, it is usually in the place of where Cognac was in the traditional version of the recipe.

CALVADOS and APPLEJACK

French Calvados is a frequently ignored base spirit with just as many possibilities as cognac. Calvados is made from apples in the same way that cognac is made from grapes. Applejack vs. Calvados is like Brandy vs. Cognac. In the same way that some brandy is better than other brandy, some applejack is better than other applejack, but no applejack is Calvados, just as no Brandy is Cognac for numerous reasons.

The differences between Calvados and American applejack are the type of apples used and the time it is aged in barrels. American applejack was originally a homemade liquor produced without distillation. Fermented apple juice was left outside in winter until it froze. Since ice is mostly water, by removing the ice, an excess of alcohol is left behind. That antiquated process is called *jacking*, and that's why it was called Applejack.

Calvados was very popular long ago, but there are very few cocktails still commonly being made with it today. Aside from the Corpse Reviver No. 1, any recipe that calls for Calvados is likely one that called for cognac originally (in the same way that a recipe calling for Armagnac is also likely to be a modification of a recipe that originally called for Cognac). Applejack has too much fresh apple taste to be very useful in making cocktails with, in the same way that apple juice is rarely a good mixer, except with Applejack!

PISCO

This is a type of brandy made in both Peru and Chile. The key differences between Brandy and Pisco are the type of grapes used (Muscat is used for all Pisco) and the lack of extensive aging for Pisco. Although some Chilean Pisco actually is aged for a relatively short time in wood barrels (3-6 months), but barrels are never used for Peruvian Pisco.

Peru has tried to argue that they alone have the right to use the name Pisco, but other countries continue to import the nearly identical product from Chile. There are two main differences. Pisco from Peru is distilled only in copper alembic stills and not diluted after the distillation, so it runs higher in alcohol. Because it is filtered anyway, they avoid the legal issues with copper ions that Cachaça has. Some Chilean Pisco is aged in wood barrels, while only glass and metal containers are allowed in Peru for aging after distillation.

Pisco from Chile is mostly distilled in stainless steel and then diluted with water to around 40% alcohol. In taste tests, the Peruvian Pisco generally wins out for quality. However, there is some fine Pisco from Chile, to be sure. One of the best examples is Waqar, which is called for in some of the recipes within this book.

TEQUILA and MEZCAL

Neither one has sugar added to it, as long as it is a quality product. The problem in creating cocktails with these distinctive Mexican spirits is that they cry out for lime juice and some kind of orange liqueur, hell bent for Margaritaville. So the vast majority of cocktails with either of these spirits is perceived as a variation of a Margarita (even when lime and orange are diligently avoided). That's not necessarily a terrible thing, though. The Margarita is one of the best cocktails in the world, and variations can be seen as unique cocktails within the framework of these base liquors.

Of the two, Mezcal is far stronger and smokier in taste. It can best be described as coarser. Until fairly recently Mezcal was more like the moonshine of Mexico, seldom exported and regarded as unsuitable for mixing. The famous worm in the bottle was something put in Mezcal for tourists as a gimmick—and never in Tequila. In recent years "artisinal" Mezcals have been marketed and trendy bars have embraced them for offering a way to go down a dirt road rather than staying on the mainstream highway, but Mezcal is an acquired taste in much the same way that Scotch is.

Both Tequila and Mezcal are made from succulents (cacti) and must contain over 50% blue agave by law. The rest can be from more than 200 other species of cacti. Quality Tequila is made from 100% blue agave in Jalisco, Mexico. That plant grows very slowly and is labor intensive to turn into the final distilled spirit. It is only made affordable by the low cost of farm labor in Mexico. If the same sort of production methods were required for Cognac, then Cognac would sell for several times as much as it does!

As in the case of all spirits, the exact flavor notes vary with the brand, the aging and the person tasting it.

WHISKEY and RYE

This category includes rye, bourbon and most whiskeys including Irish Whiskey and Canadian Whiskey, but not the one profoundly different category of Scotch Whisky (the next entry). The more pronounced the character of a base spirit is, the more difficult it is to avoid a new creation being reminiscent of a familiar standard. Just as Tequila tends to produce versions of a Margarita, any cocktail with Rye, Whiskey or Bourbon tends to come across as a version of an Old Fashioned or a Manhattan (which itself is a version of an Old Fashioned). There are some rare exceptions, but it is a formidable task to combine such a distinctive spirit with other flavors and have it be both delicious and still recognizable as whiskey in a cocktail. Therefore, whiskey cocktails are limited.

It has became somewhat popular in recent times for whiskeys to be aged in barrels previously used for other spirits, especially sherry and sometimes rum barrels. This alters the profile of the whiskey enough that it can be more easily combined with other spirits (particularly with the spirit that the barrel the whiskey was aged in). A good example of this is Teeling's Irish Whiskey aged in Rum barrels, which can be blended in cocktails with a dark rum to produce an interesting harmony.

SCOTCH WHISKY

This is arguably the most difficult of all spirits to employ in mixed drinks due to its intense and unique flavor, which is why there are so few cocktails based on Scotch. Therefore, there is little point in describing the subtle variations of Scotch within the context of this book. There is one important factor to consider, though: Most Scotch is strong with peat smoke, but a few are less so. Those few are more prone to lending themselves to working in a cocktail. My favorite for that purpose is Balvenie *DoubleWood 12 Year*. For an example, see *James and the Giant Bitch* on page 140.

OTHER SPIRITS

While there are a number of other distilled spirits that serve as the base of some cocktails such as Aquavit, Ouzo and Grappa (all previously mentioned), these are exceptions in the mainstream world of mixology. The reason is that, like smoky Scotch whisky, they have strong distinctive flavors that make them difficult to pair with other ingredients smoothly.

Having reviewed a survey of the most important ingredients, it's time to stitch all of this together into a working plan.

COCKTAIL DESIGN

When it comes to designing a new cocktail, most people are lost at sea. Here is an stepwise method for navigating that vast ocean of liquor combinations summarized in the previous chapter.

A Matter of Balance

Cocktail flavorings—that is, other than the base liquor(s)—can be arranged around a compass as shown in the diagram below. Some things do not fit in so neatly such as cream and eggs, but we will get to those things later. Here is the justification for this arrangement, moving clockwise:

1. **Alcohol** is fundamental to all cocktails. In direct opposition is dilution (water). The strength of a cocktail is an essential consideration in design. To balance a design that contains juices or tonic water, a stronger base liquor may be a answer.

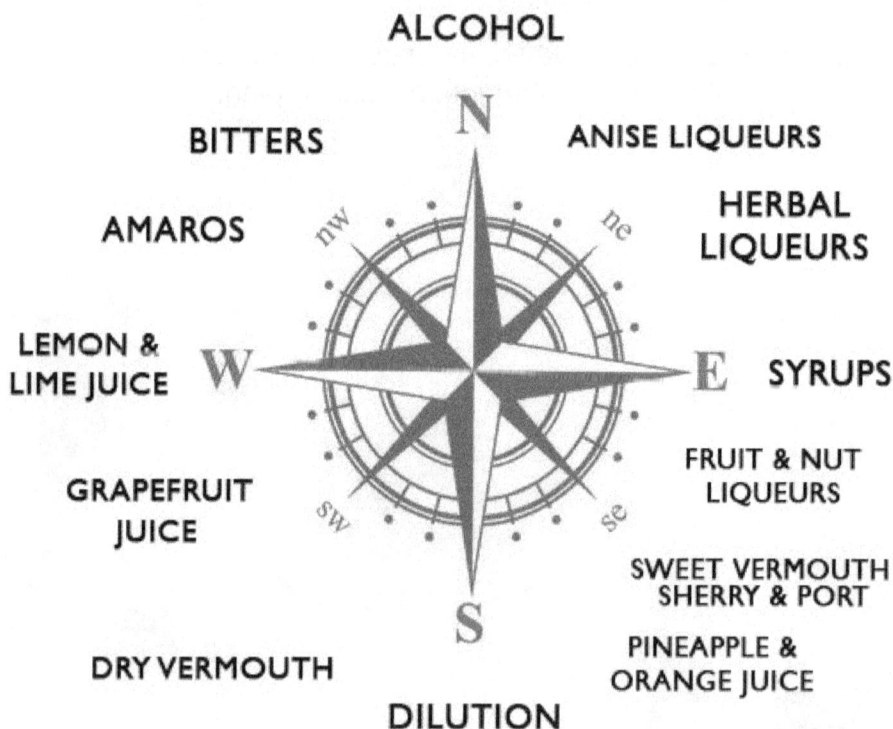

ALCOHOL

BITTERS N ANISE LIQUEURS

AMAROS nw ne HERBAL LIQUEURS

LEMON & LIME JUICE W E SYRUPS

GRAPEFRUIT JUICE sw se FRUIT & NUT LIQUEURS

SWEET VERMOUTH SHERRY & PORT

DRY VERMOUTH S PINEAPPLE & ORANGE JUICE

DILUTION

2. **Anise Liqueurs** such as absinthe are high in alcohol and intensely herbal. These can easily overpower all other ingredients, so are often used in dropwise amounts like bitters.

3. **Herbal Liqueurs** range from the sharp and strong such as Chartreuse to the sweet and mild such as Benedictine.

4. **Syrups** are flavorings that include simple sugar syrup, honey syrup, agave syrup, grenadine, falernum, orgeat, and more.

5. **Fruit and Nut Liqueurs** naturally follow orgeat and other syrups. There are dozens of liqueurs in this category. All are quite sweet and moderate in alcohol.

6. **Sweet Vermouth, Sherry & Port** are all sweet and similar in alcohol content to fruit liqueurs. In the case of sweet vermouth there are some herbal notes, which is why it is on the East side of the compass (no diagram is perfect).

7. **Pineapple and Orange Juice** are somewhat sweet, but mostly water, so they occupy the position adjacent to dilution.

8. **Dilution** is not only the addition of soda water or tonic, but also the water from ice melting into the drink. More on that later.

9. **Dry Vermouth** is a unique ingredient that doesn't fit perfectly into any one compass point, but it is mostly water, so it can be regarded as a diluting ingredient in most cocktails. Good dry vermouths have some citrus notes, especially grapefruit. They also have herbal notes, but cannot rightfully be considered an herbal liqueur.

10. **Grapefruit Juice** is mildly acidic with some slight bitter notes, thus it is on the West end of the compass, but it also dilutes some due to the high water content.

11. **Lemon & Lime Juice** are generally the only truly acidic components of a cocktail, other than Yuzu occasionally. The balance between acid and sugar are fundamental to all sweet and sour cocktails, of which there are thousands.

12. **Amari** are bitter, but they also have nuances of citrus and herbs. Some are faintly sweet, proving once again that no diagram of this sort is going to be perfect—but adding an amaro to sweeten a drink is not going to work, so I stand by my positioning of this component.

13. **Bitters** are nearly always high in alcohol and more bitter than an amaro. Just as in the case of anise liqueurs (on the opposite side of the compass), bitters are generally used in very small amounts with only a few rare exceptions such as the Trinidad Sour. Even orange bitters belong here because they are dominantly bitter in flavor and not sweet orange.

Navigation by Compass

This diagram provides some useful starting points to achieve unique and balanced recipes. Begin by selecting two opposing points on the compass. Some classic cocktails are just *that* simple, such as gin and tonic or a scotch and soda (both North + South).

This is the simplest example. First master this. Once you have selected two opposing points, choose an ingredient from each of those categories. Experiment with small amounts, keeping careful track of what the ratio seems to work best. No need to add ice. You are only evaluating the harmony of those two ingredients and determining the optimum proportions.

Now decide on a base liquor that compliments that harmonized flavor. If you aren't sure, then experiment with the mixture and several base liquors to see which one seems to work best.

Next make up a slightly larger version to stand up to ice (assuming you are not planning to serve this neat). Shake or stir with ice, as you see fit. Strain into a chilled glass, or over ice (again as you see fit). Taste it.

Now try adding a few drops of some bitters and see how that plays out. Is it better or worse? If it is worse, perhaps you have used the wrong type of bitter, or perhaps you have stumbled on an unusual case where bitters are simply not required (which is indeed rare in a three-ingredient cocktail, but it's not entirely impossible).

EXAMPLE

The following was performed randomly and recorded exactly as it happened, for better or worse. Also, it is best to work in millilitors for these tests for increased accuracy (see page 1).

1. The choice was an amaro and sweet vermouth.

2. The amaro chosen was Amaro Averna. The sweet vermouth tested was Tosti Rosso. By evaluating small portions, it seemed a ratio of 1 part amaro to 2 parts of sweet vermouth was promising.

3. A mixture of 15ml Amaro Averna, 30ml Tosti Italian Vermouth and 60ml of gin was prepared. Gin drinks are generally best stirred with ice and not shaken (see the history of James Bond on pages 49-50).

4. Tasting showed promise, but not sufficiently balanced. As a general rule of thumb, Angostura Bitters works best with cognac and whiskey cocktails (although there are many exceptions). So two dashes of Orange Bitters were added as a test. The bitters were stirred in, since that small amount will not warm the cocktail any.

5. This is suggestive of a gin long drink now. You have to go with the flow. There are shades of a Pimm's Cup.

6. For reasons of economy in the testing, Finsbury gin was used to test it so far. Now to go more in the direction of a classic summer long gin drink, it was made again using Hendrick's gin, which has notes of rose and cucumber that play well with this concept. It was stirred with ice and then poured over ice cubes in a tall glass.

7. It was still a bit lacking in sweetness for this sort of drink, so one teaspoon of the *Orange IV syrup was stirred in. This was chosen to pair with the orange bitters and the Averna. About 50ml of soda water and a thin wheel of orange was also added. This is now quite a nice and original long gin drink.

This isn't what I would call a masterpiece, but I've had far, far worse proclaimed "masterpieces" served in many bars. Using this method with just a little practice will enable you to avoid serious mishaps when creating and put you on the road to making great original drinks with very few mistakes once you get this down.

WHAT IF ?

So what if I had not decided to make this into a gin long drink? No problem! Let's keep almost everything the same. Let's swap the gin for Jim Beam Rye Whiskey. Change the orange bitters to Angostura Bitters and forget the soda water and lemon, but keep the *Orange IV syrup. Add a maraschino cherry instead of the lemon slice. Shake with ice and strain into a chilled Old Fashioned glass with a single large ice cube. Voila! Now you have a new and delicious take on a Manhattan; a cocktail that could be proudly served in any bar today.

Obviously there was some experience involved in making these decisions so easily, but the foundation was set by the compass and a few simple experiments. This method will give you a guiding light.

More Points on the Compass

Now instead of simply choosing two opposing points, let's try forming a triangle on the compass.

EXAMPLE

Once again, the following was performed randomly and recorded exactly as it happened.

1. The three-way choice was selected as pineapple/orange juice, lemon/lime juice and an herbal liqueur.

2. The specific choices made were pineapple juice, lime juice and *Tulip Cup cordial as the herbal component. Already this is screaming Tiki rum drink, but I proceeded in both the obvious way and then again with a counterintuitive path just to show that the compass is in control.

3. After a couple of experiments, it was decided that a ratio of 3:2:1 (pineapple juice, Tulip Cup Cordial and lime juice, respectively) were a good combination, balanced in sweetness with the cordial shining through. A small batch of this mixture was prepared for use in the experiments.

4. The initial choice of rum was Plantation Barbados, which is of medium density and relatively low cost. As in the previous example, it is acceptable to run tests with a lesser quality base spirit to assess the mixture. So, 22.5ml of the cordial mixture was combined with 30ml of the rum. Keep in mind that your target volume should be around 105ml for a cocktail, so 22.5 + 30 = 52.5 x 2 = 105ml, meaning this is being tested at half the volume.

5. A half dash of grapefruit bitters was added (Fee Bros.) to add some complexity. Half a dash of grapefruit bitters were chosen to match the grapefruit in the Tulip Cup Cordial. It was shaken with ice and poured over ice with a straw to test.

6. This already had the earmarks of a new Tiki style cocktail, but it could use some enhancing, so a half teaspoon of Falernum was stirred in (which would become a full teaspoon when doubled).

7. Now it was becoming quite good, with the only issue being the rum not quite standing up to the onslaught of those strong flavorings. So the experiment was repeated using a darker rum instead. Diplomático *Mantuano* was used, as it is my standard dark rum for experiments like this.

8. A tiny bit more Falernum (1/4 teaspoon) was added. Voila!

Now all that remains is to give it an intriguing Tiki name. Naming a cocktail has became very difficult lately because of the Internet. Almost any clever name you can invent has been used by someone already. But that's another topic.

WHAT IF ?

What if I swapped out the rum for a tequila? I kept everything else exactly the same. That is, 22.5ml of the 3:2:1 mixture of pineapple juice, Tulip Cup cordial and lime juice. Also the 3/4 teaspoon of falernum, and half a dash of grapefruit bitters. A blanco tequila was chosen, but I'm confident it would be fine with a reposada or even an añejo. Remember this is for a half portion, so everything would be doubled for a full serving. This was shaken with ice and strained out into a chilled glass. Both straight up and on ice were tasted. Both were delicious and neither one tasted like the one-note tequila cocktails so often served. It is not another version of a Margarita, but something all its own.

I should point out that one reason for the ease of which liquors can be swapped here is the particular choice of the Tulip Cup Cordial, which is a sort of skeleton key. That is, it tends to play well with most liquors. So does the *Unicorn Matrix Zero.

I ran yet another test after this one using vodka as the base spirit, and once again keeping everything else exactly the same except only that it was strained over a single large ice cube in a chilled Old Fashioned glass. A good result was obtained once again, but it was improved further by adding 15ml more vodka and a strip of orange peel as a garnish (rub the orange peel around the rim of the glass first). Since this is still a half portion, that would bring the total volume of the cocktail to 135ml including 90ml of vodka, which makes it a strong drink, but there are many recipes that are stronger than this.

This method will not always work, but the more you use it, the better you will get at seeing connections and making educated guesses about what to combine. It is a good set of tools, but you still have to be the mechanic.

Time is the Other Dimension

Most people do not realize that they are mostly *not* tasting the drink itself directly very much, but rather products released by enzymes in saliva that react with that drink (or food). The enzymatic reactions that produce these flavors are not instantaneous. Some reactions take longer than others, and some go through several stages, depending on what's being tasted.

The enzymes in saliva vary slightly between people due to genetics. This is why some people perceive cilantro as tasting like soap, but there are many more subtle differences. The overall ability to taste subtle flavors varies between people. That's why most people who attempt to qualify as master sommeliers fail, in spite of years of study and practice. However, you can sharpen your senses with practice using the same methods that sommeliers practice. More about that in the next section.

When you taste nearly anything, there is more than one flavor involved. Most people don't pay attention to what's going on in their mouths and sum up the entire experience in a single thought ("wine", "gin", etc.), while in reality there is an entire musical score playing if they just listened to their palate more closely.

Just as the notes in a song don't all play at the same time (or songs would sound like buzz saws and car alarms), the same goes for the flavors in foods and drinks. But especially drinks, because there is no chewing involved. Everything arrives on your tongue at the same time, ready for enzymatic processing. So cocktails are actually easier to appreciate and analyze than foods are (other than cream soups and Consommé).

The analogy between flavors and music is something useful to keep in mind when *truly* tasting anything, and not merely drinking.

✦

If life gives you lemons, make lemonade.
Then find someone whose life gave them vodka.
— Ron White

Cocktail Synthesizer ADSR

In the early days of analog music synthesizers, each key triggered a specific frequency (musical note) that was electronically shaped in an ADSR envelope. There were knobs to enable the keyboard player to set the Attack, Decay, Sustain and Release (abbreviated ADSR) *envelope*.

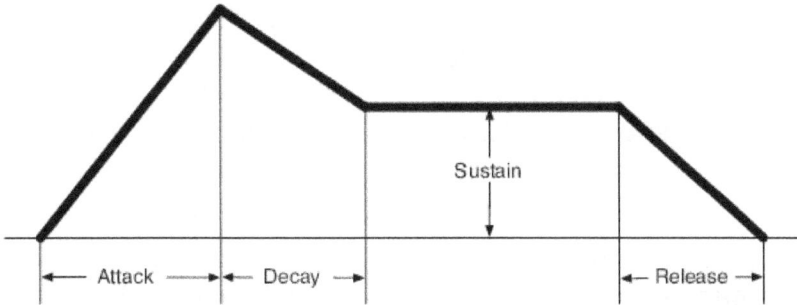

All liquors follow a similar pattern, though more complex because sound waves are two-dimensional and flavor is multi-dimensional. Still, the ADSR envelope concept is useful in trying to annotate the cascade of olfactory sensations experienced.

Just as in synthesizer music, the amount of time from the start to the finish is variable. It could be anywhere from a few seconds to a minute. The main difference with liquor and food is that you have no direct control over the settings. Your indirect control lies in your selection of ingredients and to a lesser extent, the temperature, since you can't control the nature of the ingredients themselves. In other words, you are the conductor and not the orchestra.

Just as in an orchestra, different instruments have different timbres and characteristics. When they play together, they produce chords and complex harmonies. This is the same principle involved in cocktail composition. The notes are the flavors and the tune plays itself as each component interacts with your senses in sequence. The conductor decides what sequence and how loud.

The relative amount of each liquor can be thought of as the dynamics *ppp* to *fff* in musical notation, meaning very soft to very loud. Of course, not all musical instruments are capable of both extremes. Just as in an orchestra, a

ppp pp p mp

flute playing as loudly as it can is no match for a tuba. The same is true in liquors. Fernet Branca is naturally far "louder" than vermouth, while water

mf f ff fff

can't be anything more than *molto pianissimo* (the softest possible) in terms of flavor.

Similarly, the number of notes played by each liquor on its own, and the time it takes for each little melody to play through varies wildly. The simplest example is vodka, which is as close to one note as any liquor gets. That note is simply alcohol from start to finish. Dilution turns down the volume in this analogy. Both ice and other non-alcoholic ingredients will do this, while high-proof alcohol such as Everclear will turn up the volume, but it remains that same note.

Any other spirit has more complexity than vodka. In the same way one can learn to appreciate fine wines for their subtle flavors and fleeting nuances, liquors each have their own individual characters. It's actually much easier to diagram liquors than wines because they don't change with age, there are no vintages to be concerned with—and although numerous, the number of liquors used in cocktails is far fewer than the number of wines produced.

It is very useful to keep a notebook of your personal impressions of the subtle flavors in liquors, such as the example shown on the next page. Not only will this help you to make good choices about what to combine in a cocktail you are working on designing, but it will sharpen your senses and appreciation of flavors in ways you can't even imagine until you spend some time doing it. Take a small glass of 10 to 20ml (1/3 to 2/3 ounce) of the liquor being evaluated. Smell it and record your impressions on the line marked "nose" at the bottom. Take sips and try to isolate the individual components and the stage they appear on your palate.

Write the name of the liquor at the top along with any other pertinent data. Be sure to include the date of when you evaluated it. This is an example:

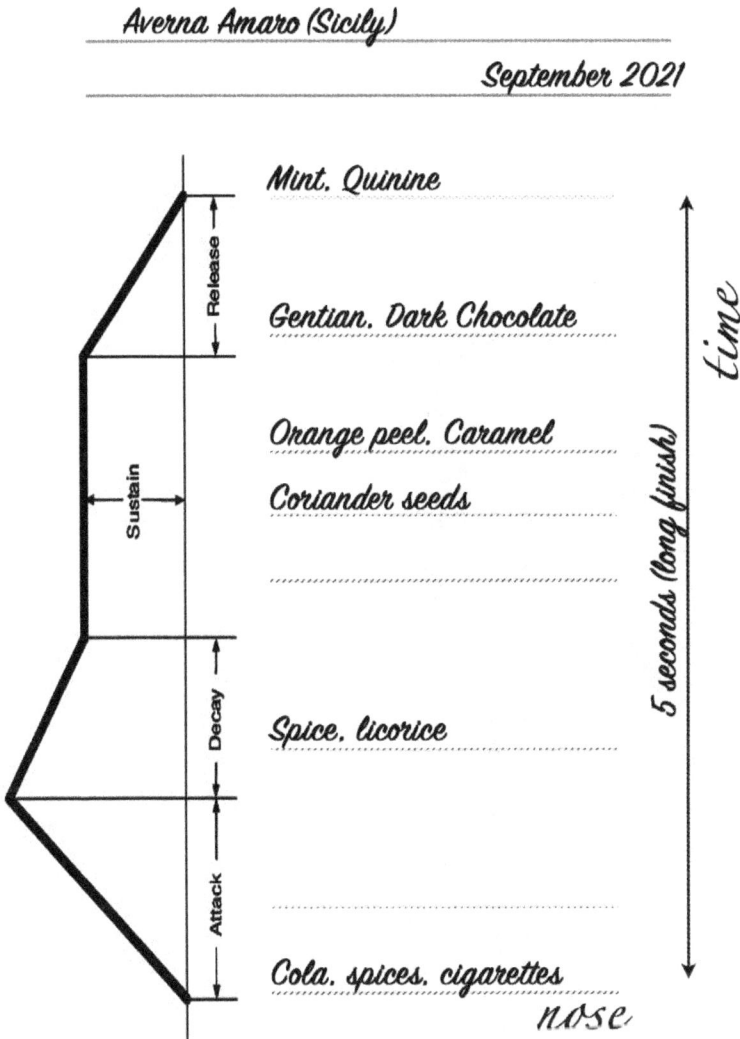

Averna Amaro (Sicily)

September 2021

Mint, Quinine

Release

Gentian, Dark Chocolate

Orange peel, Caramel

Coriander seeds

Sustain

Spice, licorice

Decay

Attack

Cola, spices, cigarettes

nose

time

5 seconds (long finish)

On the following page is a blank form that you can scan or copy by some other means as a template for your notebook file.

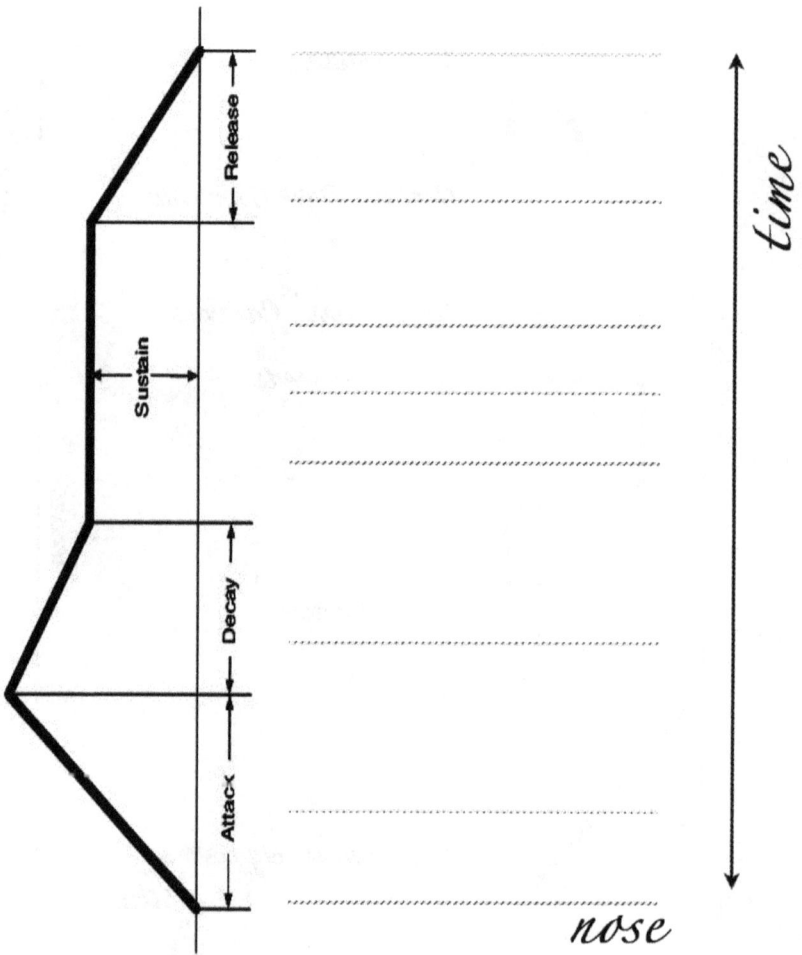

NO SPECIAL INGREDIENTS

The majority of the recipes in this book call for one or more of the homemade custom cordials and liqueurs in the appendix (recipes start on page 171), but in order to get you started, here are a few recipes that you can make with bottles right off the shelf.

Y

ONE NIGHT IN POMPEI

Theatrical and surprising in both flavor and presentation. Only slightly spicy, and with a chili to nibble on, if so desired.

45ml (1½ oz)	Gin, Tanqueray
15ml (¾ oz)	Vecchio Amaro del Cappo
15ml (¾ oz)	Cointreau
30ml (1 oz)	Orange Juice, preferably from blood oranges
1 whole	Red Chili Pepper, Serrano
1 dash	Xocolatl Mole Bitters, Bittermens
Garnish: Long Cinnamon Stick	

Leave the chili whole, but cut a small slit in one side. Do not muddle it. Combine all ingredients and stir with ice. Double strain into an Old Fashioned glass containing two large ice cubes. Fish out the red chili from the mixing glass and place it on top of the ice. Light one end of a cinnamon stick with a torch or on a gas stove. When it is smoldering red (not burning) put it into the drink with the smoking end protruding up.

PEPPER'S GHOST

The name is a play on words because of the black pepper on it. Pepper's Ghost is a common illusion and magic trick using the reflection off of glass to create a transparent "ghost" image.

60ml (2 oz)	Dark Rum, preferably Barbados
22.5ml (¾ oz)	Orange Juice
22.5ml (¾ oz)	Lemon Juice
15ml (½ oz)	Apricot Brandy, Bols
1 teaspoon	Cointreau
1 teaspoon	Ginger Liqueur, Bols
½ teaspoon	Allspice Dram, Bitter Truth

Garnish: Black Pepper, freshly ground

Combine all ingredients. Shake with ice. Strain into a chilled Old Fashioned glass with a single large ice cube. Grind some fresh black pepper over the ice.

Y

MURDER BY DEATH

A quirky cocktail for vampires and goth chicks. As you might guess from the title and the ingredients, this is *bloody* strong!

45ml (1½ oz)	Wray & Nephew Overproof Rum (126 proof)
15ml (¾ oz)	Crème de Noyaux, Tempus Fugit
2 teaspoons	Campari
2 dashes	Angostura Bitters

Garnish: Knife-point of Red Food Coloring, powdered

Combine ingredients. Stir with ice. Strain into a large chilled goblet. Add the powdered red food coloring and swirl to coat.

BENTLEY BOYS

Named after a famous British race car team and the namesake of one of the testers of cocktails within these pages, Michael Bentley.

60ml (2 oz)	Gin, Tanqueray No. Ten
15ml (½ oz)	Lemon Juice, fresh
7.5ml (¼ oz)	White Creme de Cacao
7.5ml (¼ oz)	Cointreau
½ teaspoon	Fernet Branca
¼ teaspoon	Green Chartreuse
2 thin slices	Ginger, fresh (peeled)

Garnish: Half slice of Lemon

Place the fresh ginger into the shaker. Add the lemon juice and muddle gently. Add all of the other ingredients and stir with ice. Dump the entire contents (including the slices of ginger) into a chilled lowball glass and add a straw.

REVIEW

"The Bentley Boys were a group of wealthy British motorists who enjoyed much success driving Bentley sports cars in the 1920s. The Bentley racing team scored a number of victories at this, of particular note were four consecutive victories at Le Mans (1927 - 1930). This recipe is an unusual one, presenting the paired profiles of creme de cacao and Cointreau, Fernet Branca and Green Chartreuse, lemon and ginger, with the base spirit gin providing the perfect "circuit" for these teams. There is no clear winner, in the sense that the ingredients meld quite thoroughly, which is a victory in and of itself. There is a definite spicy clement (ginger, Fernet, and even Chartreuse) playing off of a tangy counterpoint (lemon, and Chartreuse again), and the gin is beautifully present throughout. The flavors here form an elegant tangle. Surely this is the flavour of British racing green!" – Michael Bentley

TO SAUNTER

It is a great art to saunter! —Henry David Thoreau

I know of nothing else that conveys the meaning of saunter in such a liquid form as this. The strong anise liqueur is tamed some by the sweet amaretto and the bitterness of the Angostura.

60ml (2 oz)	Cognac, Pierre Ferrand *1840 1st Cru*
40ml (1.4 oz)	Amaretto DiSaronno
20ml (0.7 oz)	Pernod
7.5ml (¼ oz)	Lemon Juice
3 dashes	Angostura Bitters
Garnish: Grapefruit Peel	

Combine all ingredients. Shake with ice and then double strain into a Martini glass. Cut the grapefruit peel long. Flame it over the top and then rub it on the rim before laying the peel across the rim.

LIPSTICK THESPIAN

An heady performance by a celebrated cast. Old Tom plays it cool despite being the main character, allowing each of the others to have their moment in turn. Deserving of a standing ovation!

60ml (2 oz)	Old Tom Gin, Ableforth's *Bathtub Old Tom*
30ml (1 oz)	Cognac, Hennessy *VSOP*
30ml (1 oz)	Heering Cherry Liqueur
15ml (½ oz)	Crème de Cassis
2 dashes	Angostura Bitters

Combine all ingredients. Shake well with ice. Strain into a chilled Zombie glass filled with ice cubes. No garnish.

WESTERN WOODS

The idea of combining Rye with tonic water is more popular than many people realize. The complexity of the rich Lua coffee liqueur, slightly smoky Ancho and Jägermeister elevate this into something that is more than the sum of its parts. Consider using a 100 proof rye whiskey. The Terva Pine Liqueur is a product of Finland that is seldom seen elsewhere. The cocktail is still good without it, but this really shines like a diamond if you can include this.

60ml (2 oz)	Rye Whiskey, ideally Millstone 100
15ml (½ oz)	Ancho Reyes Ancho Chile Liqueur
15ml (½ oz)	Jägermeister
2 teaspoons	Lua Coffee Liqueur, or substitute Kahlua
1 dash	Terva Pine Tar Liqueur (see notes above)
45ml (1½ oz)	Tonic Water, Fever Tree *Mediterranean*

Combine all ingredients except the tonic water. Stir with ice cubes, then strain into a double Old Fashioned glass with a large ice cube. Add the tonic water and include a swizzle stick.

MORE ABOUT TERVA

This liqueur is a traditional Finnish product that is seldom seen elsewhere. Terva means pine tar and it is <u>very</u> *strong in flavor. If you ask someone Finnish to explain Terva, they'll tell you that it is the same stuff for patching holes in boats! There are many brands in Finland, but nowhere else that I know of. Although some liquor stores in other parts of Europe have a bottle here and there. There is also a smoked Terva that's even weirder. There are many liquors in Finland that you are unlikely to see anywhere else. Some are delicious and useful in cocktails, but I have not used any of those in the recipes in this book because they are nearly impossible to get outside of Finland. The recipe above is an exception.*

Y

QUIERO PIÑA

The name (*kee-yaroh peen-yah*) translates to "I want pineapple" in Spanish. This is based on a cocktail I saw being ordered at a bar in Chihuahua, Mexico. The customer's gruff order reminded me of the chihuahua dog in the old Taco Bell commercials saying, *Yo quiero Taco Bell* (I want Taco Bell). Since I was in Chihuahua, the name stuck with me. This recipe is my impression of what he was served. I was not given the actual recipe and the bartender did not speak English. Sometimes a starting point is all you really need. This has been designed first and foremost to be delicious with no regard for authenticity because my only clues about it were the pineapple on the rim and the grapefruit juice I saw being poured in, so I went in that direction. Normally I would have ordered one of the same drink to check out what was bringing the beaming smile to the old guy who was sipping it, but the place was closing and wouldn't open back up again until after I had to leave. There are three bitter components here, so the saline was added to temper the bitterness while retaining those flavors, as explained in an earlier chapter. Salt on the rim is optional.

45ml (1½ oz)	Tequila, Blanco (also called Silver)
30ml (1 oz)	Grapefruit Juice, fresh
22.5ml (¾ oz)	Vecchio Amaro Del Capo
7.5ml (¼ oz)	Pineapple Liqueur, DeKuyper
1 teaspoon	Saline (see page 130)
1 dash	Grapefruit Bitters, Fee Bros.
1 dash	Orange Bitters, Angostura brand

Garnishes: Fresh Pineapple Wedge and Lime Zest Spiral

Combine all ingredients. Shake very well with ice cubes. Strain into a rocks glass with ice cubes. Add the garnishes and a straw. Use fresh pineapple because canned is much too sweet.

Y

LEPRECHAUN'S LUNCH

This is a Saint Patrick's Day cocktail that I created for a place in Russia. It was later served at Laava. Admittedly it is a bit gimmicky, but appreciated by whiskey lovers. If you hate whiskey, move along.

75ml (2½ oz)	Irish Whiskey, ideally Teeling Single Malt
7.5ml (¼ oz)	Peppermint Schnapps
7.5ml (¼ oz)	Maraschino Liqueur, Luxardo
7.5ml (¼ oz)	Lime Juice
2 dashes	Aztek Chocolate Bitters, Fee Bros.

Coat the rim of a wine glass with green colored sugar. Combine all ingredients. Shake with ice. Strain into the glass.

ÉTOURDIE

The name is French for *stunned*, because that was the reaction of a French ambassador when I presented this to her. The sophistication and novelty are unexpected with so few ingredients.

45ml (1½ oz)	Gin, Beefeater
15ml (½ oz)	Bigallet China China
15ml (½ oz)	Frangelico Liqueur
15ml (½ oz)	Lemon Juice, strained
2 dashes	Orange Bitters, Angostura brand
Garnish: Orange Zest	

Combine all ingredients. Stir with ice. Strain into a chilled Coupe glass. Flame the orange zest over the top, then lay it across the edge of the glass so the guest can decide whether to add it in or not.

OLD SCATNESS

Named after an Viking settlement in Scotland. Valhalla is a
Scandinavian liqueur with the rare ability to harmonize with Scotch.

60ml (2 oz)	Scotch Whisky, Single Malt
45ml (1½ oz)	Valhalla Liqueur
2 dashes	Angostura Bitters

Garnish: Lemon Peel

*Combine all ingredients. Stir with ice. Strain into a chilled
Old Fashioned glass with a single large ice cube. Snap the
lemon peel over the drink to express the oils, then drop it in.*

Y

SWINGIN' CAT

*A man who carries a cat by the tail
learns something he can learn in no other way.*
— Mark Twain

Based on a Prohibition Era recipe from my family's Kansas City
speakeasy. The ingredients are much better quality now, of course.

60ml (2 oz)	Bathtub Gin, Ableforth's (see page 139)
30ml (1 oz)	Cointreau
22.5ml (¾ oz)	Madeira, Blandy's 5 Year
7.5ml (¼ oz)	Lemon Juice, strained
2 dashes	Boker's Bitters

Garnish: Orange Peel

*Rub the rim of a Coupe glass with the orange peel. Combine
all ingredients and stir with ice. Strain into the glass.*

GAUDI

Antoni Gaudi was the amazing Art Noveau architect of Barcelona. This cocktail is a liquid adventure! Remarkable for being so simple. Dry, yet sweet, with abstract curves. This specific sherry is the key.

45ml (1½ oz)	Sherry, Osborne *VORS Amontillado 51-1A*
45ml (1½ oz)	Vodka, Russian Standard was used
30ml (1 oz)	Amaretto DiSaronno
7.5ml (¼ oz)	Lemon Juice, strained
2 dashes	Angostura Bitters

Combine all ingredients and shake with ice. Strain over two large ice cubes in a rocks glass. Inhale and sip slowly.

Y

G SHARP

A derivative of my Gaudi cocktail (see above). This one was first auditioned to a group of musicians about to perform at a nightclub I was bartending at. The girl singer, who was used to candy-sweet cocktails, winced, stammering, "Geez...sharp!" The guitarist gulped about half of it down in a single swallow and cleverly replied, "Nah. It's an A Flat." For non-musicians, G sharp and A flat are the same note. It had less lime juice originally, as noted in the recipe.

50ml (1¾ oz)	Torres 10 Spanish Brandy (don't use cognac)
40ml (1.4 oz)	Amaretto DiSaronno
22.5ml (¾ oz)	Lime Juice, strained (originally 15ml or ½ oz)
7.5ml (¼ oz)	White Crème de Menthe, Tempus Fugit
3 dashes	Bergamot Bitters

Combine all ingredients and shake with ice. Strain into a rocks glass with fresh ice cubes. Add a straw.

ROMANZA

The name means *romance* in Italian. Grappa is one of the most challenging liquors to integrate smoothly into a cocktail, but it does pair well with coffee, cream and almonds. It is important to use Columbian rum in this, and most especially Dictador because the terroir of the coffee beans growing near the sugarcane permeates the flavor of the rum. While you can use other coffee liqueurs here, Lua is a deep, rich liqueur that is vastly superior to any other that I know of. This is related to an after dinner drink with coffee, rum and cream served at Trader Vic's long ago, but honestly this is much more complex and alluring.

30ml (1 oz)	Grappa, Il Moscato di Nonino
22.5ml (¾ oz)	Columbian Rum, Dictador
15ml (½ oz)	Lua Licor de Café, or substitute Kahlua
15ml (½ oz)	Amaretto DiSaronno
15ml (½ oz)	Heavy Cream
¼ teaspoon	Orange Zest, grated (see directions below)

Garnish: Orange Peel, Freshly grated Nutmeg

Grate the orange zest over a fine mesh sieve. Pour the grappa over the orange zest into a shaker, pressing down on the zest to express as much of the liquor as possible. Then discard the zest. Add the rest of the ingredients and shake with ice. Double strain into a chilled Coupe glass. Rub the rim with the orange peel, then discard it. Finely grate nutmeg over the top.

Y

"A romance is a moderately written play with a badly written third act."
— Truman Capote

GRAPEFRUIT TONIC HIGHBALL

This is a curious combination that tastes more like grapefruit than it has a right to. A wonderful alternative to a Mimosa with brunch.

60ml (2 oz)	Vodka
22.5ml (¾ oz)	Crème de Cassis, Marie Brizard
15ml (½ oz)	Kirschwasser, Schwarzwälder
2 teaspoons	Lime Juice, or 1 teaspoon Yuzu Juice
7.5ml (¼ oz)	Pimento Dram, The Bitter Truth
3-4 dashes	Grapefruit Bitters, Fee Bros.
60ml (2 oz)	Tonic Water, Fever Tree *Indian*

Garnish: Grapefruit Peel

Use a vegetable peeler to cut a long strip of the grapefruit peel. Wrap it around a chopstick or metal straw to curl it. Combine all of the ingredients except the grapefruit bitters and the tonic water in a shaker. Rock back and forth with ice cubes for 15 seconds. Dump contents into a Highball glass to fill. Sprinkle the grapefruit bitters on top, then add the grapefruit peel and a straw.

BRIAN'S SAUCE

A sweetened Martini for Family Guy's most unusual dog.

30ml (1 oz)	Gin, Bombay Sapphire
30ml (1 oz)	Light Rum, Havana Club 3 Year
15ml (½ oz)	Dry Vermouth
1 teaspoon	Simple Syrup (1:1 ratio)

Garnish: Olive on a skewer (decoration only, incompatible flavor)

Shake with ice. Strain into a Martini glass. Add olive.

HARA SAPANA

The name means *green dream* in Hindi. As you may know, Britain, a nation that was famously joked about for bland food, has fallen in love with their version of Indian curries. This is a London Dry Gin cocktail that is quite spicy. It makes a smashing cocktail to accompany samosas as an appetizer. Beer for the rest of the meal!

60ml (2 oz)	Gin, Tanqueray
15ml (½ oz)	Lime Juice
7.5ml (¼ oz)	Suze Gentian Liqueur
7.5ml (¼ oz)	Grand Marnier
¼ teaspoon	Olive Oil, high quality extra-virgin

Also: Fresh Coriander (Cilantro Stems), Green Serrano Chili

Remove the stem from the chili and cut <u>half</u> of it into slices. Add to a shaker with the gin and a few cilantro stems. Muddle. Add the other ingredients except the olive oil. Shake with ice. Double strain into a chilled Martini glass. Add the olive oil.

Y

KITCHEN CINCO DE MAYO

A customer asked for something original and named his favorite spirits. I poured all of then into a shaker and added some bitters. The result was very good after a few adjustments. See for yourself!

50ml (1¾ oz)	Tequila, Reposado
30ml (1 oz)	Jägermeister
7.5ml (¼ oz)	Anisette Liqueur, Marie Brizard
7.5ml (¼ oz)	Apricot Liqueur, Merlet
4 dashes	Xocolatl Mole Bitters, Bittermens

Shake everything with ice. Strain into a chilled Coupe glass.

A SENSE OF DOUBT

Although the brown color may inspire a sense of doubt, this was one of my contest winners. Try it and see why.

45ml (1½ oz)	Brandy, ideally Torres 10 *Double Barrel*
22.5ml (¾ oz)	*Cloudy Pear Vodka or Absolut Pears Vodka
15ml (½ oz)	Lemon Juice
15ml (½ oz)	*The Other* Grenadine
Also: Orange Peel, Blended non-smoky Scotch (see below)	

Rinse a chilled Coupe glass with a half teaspoon of blended Scotch. Combine all of the ingredients and shake with ice cubes. Strain into the glass. Flame the orange peel over the top.

Y

TRAILING BY A FURLONG

A ridiculously long finish. The hazelnut flavor is barely noticeable while sipping this, but eventually the Frangelico finally crosses the finish line. The quinine-like astringency that follows is especially interesting as it compels you to quench your thirst with yet another.

60ml (2 oz)	Gin, Tanqueray No. Ten or (better) Rangpur
30ml (1 oz)	Frangelico
15ml (½ oz)	Grapefruit Juice
7.5ml (¼ oz)	Yuzu Juice
½ teaspoon	Heering Cherry Liqueur
½ teaspoon	Grapefruit Zest, grated (see directions below)

Grate the grapefruit zest onto a metal sieve. Pour the gin over it slowly. Press down to express the oils. Discard the zest. Add the other ingredients. Stir with ice. Strain into a chilled Martini glass.

KŪIKAWĀ

Here's a cocktail that segues perfectly into the next section. It contains no specially prepared ingredients, and is very much in the style of a classic Trader Vic cocktail (even though the ingredients are rather unorthodox from Vic's typical arsenal). The name means *something special* in Hawaiian.

45ml (1½ oz)	Calvados
30ml (1 oz)	Heering Cherry Liqueur
30ml (1 oz)	Pomegranate Juice, fresh (see note below)
4 dashes	Orange Bitters, Angostura brand
6-8 drops	Vanilla Extract
1 teaspoon	Overproof Rum, Plantation *OFTD*

Garnishes: Pineapple and cherry on a skewer.

Combine all ingredients except the overproof rum. Shake well with ice cubes, or flash blend, then dump the contents into a Highball glass. Float the rum. Add the garnish. Stick a paper umbrella pick into the pineapple and add a straw.

POMEGRANATE JUICE

Put the seeds and pulp of the fruit into a food processor and purée as best as possible. Do not use a blender for this or it will be cloudy. Pass the contents first through a coarse sieve and then through the finest mesh of a tamis. Refrigerate and it will keep for a week.

REVIEWS

"Nice color. The first whiff is Cherry Heering but with the fresh pomegranate it's smooth. The flavor profile is complex. I taste apple, pomegranate...cherry. Rolling over the tongue, I feel somewhat of a cooling, almost numbing sensation. Strikes me as a very Autumnal drink. Pretty smooth start with a drier, almost tart finish. My wife says it reminds her of Christmas." — Shane Hawkins-Wilding

Y

Tropical Cocktails

Most people are unaware that the name *Tiki* is the name of the first man in the Maori religion (akin to Adam in the Bible). There is a growing resentment among native Hawaiians over what they see as cultural appropriation, and so they prefer the term Tropical to Tiki when it comes to restaurants and cocktails. Not to get political here, but I can't help but point out the paradoxical nature of their fundamental argument: That western Tiki culture has nothing to do with their native religion, and yet at the same time they feel that it is cultural appropriation. I'll just leave it at that.

Tropical is an umbrella term including both traditional Tiki drinks as well as cocktails from the Caribbean and South America. The latter two evolved independently from the Tiki roots of Trader Vic and Don the Beachcomber, naturally. They share many of the same attributes, though. Namely being primarily sweet and sour cocktails that include fruit juice and usually rum. Tiki drinks tend to be much more complex—especially if you know the complete recipes, which are often kept secret with only a rough outline of the ingredients ever being published. I covered that topic in detail in my previous *Cocktails of the South Pacific* book.

That's not to say that Tiki cocktails have a monopoly on complex recipes, especially in this age of artisanal bars trying to justify high prices and cultivate a following for drinks you can only get there. Many cocktails have many more ingredients than people usually consider. Take the classic Negroni, for instance. It contains just three ingredients: Gin, Campari and Italian Vermouth. Yet each of those ingredients contains dozens of herbs and citrus peels. It is poured out of only three bottles, but the complex taste is due to all of the ingredients that went into those liquors.

Most bars and bar owners prefer cocktails with only three or four ingredients. They are fast to make, easy to memorize and easy to understand for the guest. Such cocktails are not for the adventurous—and adventure is the hallmark of true Tikidom. Although admitedly it is all relative, and even a Daiquiri is an "adventure" for someone who routinely orders a Rum and Coke.

If there is one thing that can't be disputed about Donn Beach, it was invention of the "Kaleidoscope of Colors and Flavors" that he brought to cocktails. Prior to him, nearly every cocktail was either clear or brown and served in simple ordinary glassware. In the world of cocktails, he was like the first color television set that could get more than three channels.

However, when it came to the culture and lore of Tiki, there was no one like Trader Vic to romanticize the South Seas and capitalize on a restaurant's ambience. The fact that rum came from the opposite side of the planet from Polynesia was glossed over. The truth is that sweet and sour rum drinks originated in the Caribbean centuries before Tiki was a thing. It should also be noted that we can thank Robert Louis Stevenson's iconic book, *Treasure Island*, for convincing us that pirates thrived on rum. In fact it was the English Navy that was given rum, while most pirates preferred the refined taste of cognac. But, "Yo, ho, ho and a bottle of Hennessy" doesn't have quite the same ring to it.

Ultimately, Tiki was created as a sort of Disneyland dark ride involving sugary liquors, topless native girls, tikis and pirate ships.

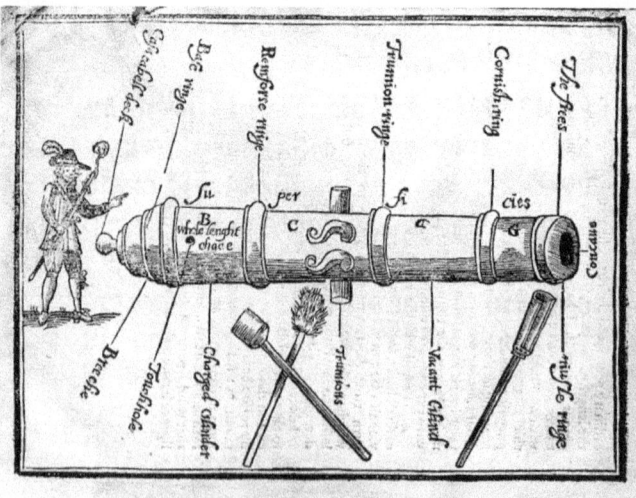

AVERY'S 62 CANNONS

A flamboyant cocktail with fiery style. Captain Avery came to command *The Fancy* after a mutiny. At a time when ships had around 30 cannons, he reconfigured his to have 62 and made other revolutionary changes to make his ship fast and maneuverable. Eventually he retired and was one of the very few pirates who managed to evade capture, even after a decade long manhunt.

This is is a wild cocktail full of fire and ash reminiscent of the smoking 62 cannons blazing on *The Fancy*. It was designed for Don Giovanni's Mandarino liqueur from Italy, but since this is going to be difficult for most people to get, you can substitute Mandarine Napoleon with fairly good results—but it won't be quite the same.

45ml (1½ oz)	Barbados Rum, ideally 1731 Fine & Rare 8 Year
2 teaspoons	151-proof Rum, ideally Tilambic from Mauritius
30ml (1 oz)	Aperol
22.5ml (¾ oz)	Mandarino, Don Giovanni (see text above)
30ml (1 oz)	Lime Juice
2 dashes	Xocolatl Molé Bitters, Bittermens

Garnish: Cinnamon Stick, Sugar, Lime Shell (see directions)

Put about 130 grams (4 ½ oz) of crushed ice into a heavy goblet. Add all of the other ingredients to the glass and stir. Now place the lime shell on top of the ice, hollowed-side up. Sprinkle on about ¾ teaspoon of granulated sugar. Then add the 151-proof rum on the sugar. Set a long cinnamon stick ablaze with a blowtorch or gas stove. Use the flame on the cinnamon to light the rum in the lime shell, holding it over the lime to increase the flame. After a short time, extinguish the fire by pushing the lime down into the drink with the cinnamon. The black burnt cinnamon is part of the flavor. Now you can safely add a straw.

Y

86

THE CALL OF ADVENTURE

Classic Tiki flavor, but this cocktail will be a murky brown without food color. That's not an issue when served in an opaque ceramic Tiki mug, but if you are putting it in a clear glass goblet, it will be rather ugly without some "makeup". Be careful to only use a tiny bit, especially if you are using the powdered kind (which is better) or you will have the cocktail equivalent of Tammy Faye Bakker.

30ml (1 oz)	Dark Rum, Diplomático *Mantuano*
30ml (1 oz)	Barbados Rum
30ml (1 oz)	Banana Liqueur, Tempus Fugit
22.5ml (¾ oz)	Orange Juice
15ml (½ oz)	Lime Juice
2 dashes	Orange Bitters, Angostura brand
pinch	Orange and/or Yellow Food Color (optional)

Garnishes: Mint, Lime Wheel, Luxardo Cherry

Shake with ice and then dump into a Tiki mug. Add a spray of freshly picked mint (or spearmint) and a straw. Fold the lime wheel in half around the cherry and secure with a skewer. Lay the skewer across the top of the cocktail.

REVIEWS

"Well, this one does not taste the way I expected it to! The orange and lime are thoro, but in minor roles, and I feel like the banana is strongly pointing to the rums, so the overall profile is not overly sweet and is skewed towards the alcohol, which is quite interesting. As dilution sets in the fruit emerges on the palette, almost as an after taste, hints of the orange, banana, and lime. A lot of ice is probably key here, but get the drink cold in the shaker. For me larger cubes in the shaker work well to cool, but not over dilute." – Michael Bentley

"Subbed El Dorado 12 as the dark rum, as it fit best what I have in stock. Simple and straightforward, allowing both the complex rum and rich banana liqueur to shine through its tasty framework. Adventure awaits!" – Craig Carpel

DOUBLOONS IN JUNE

The vanilla notes of the terroir in this rum from Madagascar make this blend special, but you can use another dark rum if need be.

65ml (2.3 oz)	Dark Rhum, preferably Dzama *Cuvée Noire*
22.5ml (¾ oz)	*Bramble Liqueur
15ml (½ oz)	D.O.M. Benedictine
15ml (½ oz)	Lime Juice
1 teaspoon	*Vic's Rum Nastoyka
3-4 drops	Vanilla Extract

Garnishes: Two Kumquat Wheels, gold sugar (see text below)

Fill a double rocks glass with ice cubes. Combine all ingredients. Shake with ice and strain into the glass. Dust the kumquat wheels with metallic gold or bronze sugar (as used in cake decorations) and lay them on top.

$$\math128Y$$

RUM, GLORIOUS RUM!

This expresses of the best qualities of the best rum. My personal favorite here is Mezan *XO* Jamaican Rum, which really sings! The Mai Tai rum copy (page 104) is also something to experience.

75ml (2 ½ oz)	Top Shelf Rum (see notes above)
15ml (½ oz)	*Orange IV Syrup
7.5ml (¼ oz)	Apricot Brandy (not liqueur)
7.5ml (¼ oz)	*Bramble Liqueur
7.5ml (¼ oz)	Lime Juice

Shake with ice, then strain into a lowball glass with a single large ice cube. No garnish.

RUM IDOLATRY

In spite of the many ingredients, this recipe has been included here because it is worth the trouble, especially for a devoted Tiki afficionado. Note that a big part of the success of this cocktail lies in the rum float. My favorite by far for this is Opthimus *25 Años Solera* OportO Ron Artesanal from the Dominican Republic, but choose a highly aromatic rum in any case.

45ml (1½ oz)	Light Rum, Plantation 3-Star
30ml (1 oz)	Pineapple Juice
15ml (½ oz)	*Royal Scandinavian Cordial
15ml (½ oz)	Lime Juice
7.5ml (¼ oz)	Grand Marnier
7.5ml (¼ oz)	*Sicilian Bitter Lemon Cordial
7.5ml (¼ oz)	Pimento Dram, The Bitter Truth
¾ teaspoon	Jägermeister
2 dashes	Elemakule Bitters, Bittermens
2 teaspoons	Overproof Aged Rum (see text above)

Garnishes: Luxardo Cherry and an Edible Flower

Combine all ingredients except the dark rum. Shake with ice. Strain into a Highball glass or a Tiki mug partially filled with ice cubes. Add more ice if needed. Float the dark rum. Thread the cherry on a skewer and lay across the top along with the flower. Add a straw and serve.

GIN IDOLATRY

As a variation, you can mix up the same ingredients but with Kyrö *Napue* gin in place of the light rum, grapefruit bitters in place of the Elemakule bitters, and the float being Tanqueray No. Ten gin.

Y

20 LASHES

Here is another application of Calvados (see page 55) – and it's only a punishment if you fail to use enough cracked ice!

45ml (1 ½ oz)	Overproof Dark Rum, Plantation *OFTD*
15ml (½ oz)	*Falernum
15ml (½ oz)	Lime Juice
15ml (½ oz)	Calvados
15ml (½ oz)	Grand Marnier
1 dash	Bittermens Elemakule bitters

Garnishes: Mint, Lime Wheel, Luxardo Cherry

Combine ingredients in a shaker. Add a copious amount of cracked ice. Shake briefly then dump into a Tiki mug. Add the lime wheel and cherry on a skewer along with the mint and a straw.

REVIEWS

"The profile is that of a Caribbean punch where the falernum, lime, and Tiki bitters set the course, and the wonderful OFTD and Calvados drive the ship ahead. Rum forward and strong!" — Michael Bentley

AYE, THE PRISONER LOOKS VERY NICE - BUT THATS NOT WHAT I MEANT BY 20 LASHES.

"It is bright and citrusy with subtle cinnamon and clove notes from the Elemakule bitters. A perfect balance of citrus and sweet. Not too strong, a great drink for a warm & sunny day! 5 stars!! " — Sherri Rowland

"20 lashes! The beatings will continue until morale improves! Of note: The first quaff will put hair on your chest." — Shane Hawkins-Wilding

ANGRY WITCHDOCTOR

You might be angry if someone put hot sauce in your rum cocktail, too. Or maybe you wouldn't... This is strong and spicy! Properly warned, ye be, says I. As for the rum, this is a rare instance where Clairin is used. In case Clairin is new to you, it is a rum from Haiti that has so much funk and grassy notes that most Martinique agricole rhums pale in comparison. Clairin is made from pure sugarcane juice and it is naturally fermented without the addition of cultured yeast. See pages 50-52 on how various rums are produced. Clairin is used in voodoo rituals there. Because there are no real government regulations, a lot of Clairin is what we might call amateur moonshine. It is produced *by* and *for* locals only. The exported product is actually safe for consumption (don't worry)—but the taste might make you wonder about that.

If you have the budget and ability to find it, a better choice for this cocktail is Ghana limited edition Rom de Luxe (shown in the photo). It has much of the same unusual character as Clairin, but is smoother and without the strange aftertaste that you may object to. In this cocktail, the massive hit of Grand Marnier coupled with the hot spice mask the unpleasant notes to make for a real rum adventure.

50ml (1¾ oz)	Clairin or Ghana Rum (see text above)
45ml (1½ oz)	Grand Marnier
30ml (1 oz)	Lime Juice
3 dashes	Xocolatl Mole Bitters, Bittermens
1 dash	Tabasco Sauce

Shake with ice and then strain into either an appropriate Tiki mug or a chilled lowball glass with a lot of ice cubes. Serve with a straw.

CUBAN WITCHDOCTOR

This is what you get when you cross an Angry Witchdoctor with a laid back Cuban sipping a Daiquiri. Haiti lies directly southeast of Cuba, sharing the island with the Dominican Republic just a bit further east. All three nations are excellent rum producers. Unlike the Angry Witchdoctor on the previous page, the Haitian rum in this one needs to be the more refined type rather than the rougher Clairin type. The two that I would recommend the most are Plantation *XO Haiti* (which is really the best), or Compagne des Indies *Haiti 11 ans* (aged 11 years). Unfortunately both are scarce and rather expensive as rums go. Barbancourt is also acceptable.

As for the Cuban rum, while Havana Club 7 would be the usual choice, step up your game to Ron Mulata 15 Year (also from Cuba), if you can. If you can't get Cuban Rum, Matusalem 7 Year Solera is extremely similar to Havana Club 7 Year.

22.5ml (¾ oz)	Dark Cuban Rum (see text above)
22.5ml (¾ oz)	Haitian Rum (see text above)
15ml (½ oz)	Light Rum, Plantation 3-Star
15ml (½ oz)	Pineapple Juice
15ml (½ oz)	*Tulip Cup Cordial
15ml (½ oz)	Lime Juice
1 teaspoon	Maraschino Liqueur
2 dashes	Bergamot Bitters

Garnishes: Pineapple Fronds, Mint

Shake everything with ice and then strain into either a chilled lowball glass or (better) some kind of crazy Tiki mug with ice cubes. Add pineapple fronds and a sprig of fresh spearmint. Serve with a straw.

Y

ZUMBIDO LIBIDO

Zumbido means *buzzing* in Spanish, a reference to the honey in this. Not all honey is created the same. You need a strong tasting honey here or you won't taste the honey at all. Increasing the amount will make it too sweet. This recipe is the result of dozens of experiments to achieve a mix with a unique taste and many layers of flavors. This giant long recipe is one that bartenders hated!

45ml (1½ oz)	Dark Rum, Havana Club 7 (see text below)
2 teaspoons	Jamaican Rum, Smith & Cross
30ml (1 oz)	Orange Juice
15ml (½ oz)	Lime Juice
15ml (½ oz)	Honey Syrup (50% water)
1 teaspoon	*Bramble Liqueur
1 teaspoon	D.O.M. Benedictine
1 teaspoon	Apricot Brandy (not liqueur)
1 dash	Orange Bitters, Fee Bros.
3-4 drops	Orange Blossom Water

Garnishes: Lime Wedge and Spearmint

Combine all ingredients and shake with ice cubes. Dump the contents into a chilled Tiki mug and garnish with a wad of spearmint. Slice the lime wedge onto the rim. Add a straw.

SUBSTITUTIONS

Havana Club 7: As in the case of the Cuban Witchdoctor recipe on the previous page, you can substitute Matusalem 7 Year Solera for the Havana Club 7 with identical results.

Smith & Cross: Although not as intense, Mezan Jamaica XO is quite good in this. If you combine it 1:1 with Plantation OFTD rum, so much the better. If you have nothing else, you can use straight OFTD.

LITTLE GRASS SHACK

This was named after a popular 1933 Hawaiian song. It was on menus in Hawaii back in the 1940's, but seems to have been completely forgotten. Probably due to Okolehao (a unique Hawaiian distilled spirit) being something that very few bars stock. You can make this with Pisco and still have a nice tropical drink, though. The amount of lime juice may need to be adjusted to suit your taste.

45ml (1½ oz)	Okolehao, or Pisco (see text above)
22.5ml (¾ oz)	Pisang Liqueur, DeKuyper
15ml (½ oz)	Lime Juice, strained
2 teaspoons	Green Crème de Menthe, DeKuyper
7.5ml (¼ oz)	Apricot Brandy, Bols

Garnishes: Lime Wedge, Paper Umbrella

Combine everything and shake with ice. Strain into either a chilled Coupe glass to serve straight up, or in a rocks glass with ice cubes or crushed ice and a straw. Add lime and umbrella.

Y

SIX BELLS

...the 3:00am watch shift begins on a freighter. This is a cocktail to savor as the segue between rum and a long night of coffee.

45ml (1½ oz)	Light Rum, Plantation 3-Star
15ml (½ oz)	Columbian Rum, ideally Dictador *XO*
15ml (½ oz)	Lime Juice
15ml (½ oz)	Espresso Coffee, cold
15ml (½ oz)	*Earth Tones Cordial
7.5ml (¼ oz)	*Falernum

Shake all ingredients with ice. Strain into a rocks glass.

COLUMBIA TE CANTO

The name is Spanish for, "Columbia, I sing to you!" Aside from being the title of a masterpiece in salsa music by Eddie Palmieri, this is all about the Columbian rum. Although you *can* make this with any dark rum, an aged Dictador Columbian rum will make this something special. Columbian rum has strong notes of coffee from the terroir, just as Madagascar rums have vanilla notes. My choice is Dictador *XO Solera Perpetual* rum for this, but it is rare and expensive. The 16 Year Dictador is nearly as good. While many rum enthusiasts say it's a crime against nature to mix with such a fine sipping rum into a cocktail, the fact is that top shelf ingredients always shine through, just as cheap ingredients ruin everything.

60ml (2 oz)	Dark Rum, Columbian (see text above)
22.5ml (¾ oz)	*Light Coconut Syrup
15ml (½ oz)	*Apricot Cognac or Apricot Brandy
15ml (½ oz)	Apricot Liqueur, Merlet
15ml (½ oz)	Lime Juice
7.5g (¼ oz)	*Old Fashioned Orgeat
1 teaspoon	Suze Gentian Liqueur

Shake everything with ice and then strain into a rocks glass with cracked ice. Serve with a straw.

Y

MORE ABOUT EDDIE PALMIERI

At one point in the 1960's Palmieri was so prolific and so popular, that in parts of South America there were record stores that only sold his recordings—nothing else!—and they had enough business to keep going like that for years. In 1971, Palmieri decided he would shift gears from quantity to quality. For the next seven years he worked on his groundbreaking album that would be called *Lucumi, Macumba, Voodoo* (three types of voodoo). *Columbia te Canto* is arguably the best track. The life lesson here is to have at least one masterpiece in your life that you devote yourself to.

LAND HO!

The star of this cocktail is the aroma of the rum from Réunion (a tiny island off the coast of Madagascar). The rum from there is unique, as are most regional rums due to the variety of materials and methods (pages 50-52). Rum Nation's *Reunion 7 Year* (which is 126 proof) is hard to find and expensive, but the aroma is intense, which is why it is floated on the lime shell here rather than being mixed into the cocktail where it would be lost among the ice cubes and other ingredients.

On close inspection, you may see similarities in the "skeleton" of this recipe with the Columbia Te Canto recipe on the previous page. Both have gentian (Suze in that one and Amaro di Angostura here); Both have a potent rum component (Dictador Columbian there and Rum Nation Reunion here). These similarities are not by chance. Once a successful structure has been worked out, often a new cocktail that is just as well balanced and interesting can be derived by switching things around a bit and experimenting. You can use Plantation OFTD in place of a Reunion rum here, but that makes it sweeter and not nearly as fragrant.

45ml (1½ oz)	Light Rum, Plantation 3-Star
22.5ml (¾ oz)	Pisang, DeKuyper
22.5ml (¾ oz)	Amaro di Angostura
15ml (½ oz)	*Homemade Macadamia Nut Rum
22.5ml (¾ oz)	Lime Juice
1 dash	Black Walnut Bitters, Fee Bros.
1 teaspoon	Overproof Rum, ideally Réunion (see text)

Garnishes: Half of a Lime Shell (pirate flag on toothpick optional)

Combine everything except the overproof rum. Shake with ice and then strain into a Tiki mug containing cracked ice. Add the lime shell (cut-side down) for the "island". Drizzle overproof rum over the shell for aroma. Add a straw.

Y

THE NAVIGATOR'S BALLS

The "navigator's balls" is old sailor's slang for a binnacle, which is used in navigation and has two large steel balls on either side (one red and one green, thus the red and green maraschino cherry garnish) — and this does have some real balls for those not accustomed to the strong taste of agricole rhum. You can substitute another dark rum if you are not a fan of it. In the same way that magic happens with the rum float in the *Land Ho!* cocktail, the same goes here. My favorite for this one is S.B.S. *Panama 2006* (at 119 proof), but it is quite scarce so you will probably have to find your own jewel to crown this one with. Finally, note that while the Tulip Cup Cordial is only a small part by volume, it is essential to the recipe.

45ml (1½ oz)	Martinique Rum, or other Dark Rum
22.5ml (¾ oz)	Lime Juice
15ml (½ oz)	Pomegranate Juice, fresh (see page 83)
15ml (½ oz)	*The Other* Grenadine
15g (½ oz)	Mango Purée (see below)
7.5g (¼ oz)	*Tulip Cup Cordial
1 dash	Angostura Bitters
1-2 teaspoons	Overproof Rum (see text above)
Garnishes: A Red and a Green Maraschino Cherry	

*Combine everything but the overproof rum. Shake with ice and then strain into a Tiki mug with **cracked ice**. Float the overproof rum and add the cherries on a skewer and a straw.*

MANGO PURÉE

Combined equal parts (by weight) of freshly peeled ripe mango flesh, sugar and water in a blender. Blend until smooth, then rub it through the second most coarse mesh sieve of a tamis or other relatively coarse sieve. Weigh the resulting purée and add 5% (by weight) of lemon juice. This is thinner than some purées, but thicker than syrup. Refrigerate!

Y

RUSTY ANCHOR

The crux of this cocktail is the rum, as should be the case in any truly Tiki cocktail. An intense rum such as Hamilton 86 or Smith and Cross is well suited, but you may want to try this with the imitation of Wray & Nephew 17 Year, too (see page 104).

60ml (2 oz)	Dark Rum, ideally Hamilton 86
30ml (1 oz)	Orange Juice, fresh
15ml (½ oz)	Lime Juice, fresh
15ml (½ oz)	D.O.M. Benedictine
15g (½ oz)	Mango Purée (see bottom of previous page)
1 dash	Cardamom Bitters, Fee Bros.

Combine all ingredients. Shake with ice cubes and then strain over plenty of crushed ice into a chilled Collins glass.

REVIEWS

"I made the Rusty Anchor tonight, and it was a success. I found a few interesting things here. First of all, I'm impressed that the relatively small quantity of mango stands up to the strong flavors of the Benedictine and the rum (I used the Hamilton 86, as suggested), I thought it might get overwhelmed. I'm also fascinated to say that somewhere in the middle of the drink (middle of my consumption, mid point in dilution) there appeared another coherent flavor that I cannot quite identify. It's fruit, reasonably bright… almost like peach or nectarine? I am now wondering if the cardamom bitters are a contributor to this. Well, that's the magic of good mixology!" — Michael Bentley

"This surprised me from the common Tiki ingredients to deliver such a unique flavor with different kinds of tastes coming at you in turns and then finishing with something mysterious that makes you go back for more. When I mixed this, the vapors made me think it would be much too strong, but after it is stirred with all the crushed ice, it is just perfect!" — Karlo Hautamäki

Y

"It's more fun to be a pirate than to join the navy." — Steve Jobs

FIRE EATERS OF MARACAIBO

One of the hallmarks of theatrical Tropical cocktails is fire. Along the beaches of Maracaibo in Venezuela there are fire eaters performing at night to entertain tourists. Naturally Venezuelan rum is the main spirit in this. Maracaibo is on the historic Spanish Main, home to pirates and many a tale of buried treasure.

60ml (2 oz)	Rum, Diplomático *Reserva Exclusiva*
30ml (1 oz)	*Golden Lime Cordial
22.5ml (¾ oz)	Apricot Brandy (not liqueur)
15ml (½ oz)	Lime Juice, fresh
2 teaspoons	Mezcal, ideally Cuish Belato
7.5ml (¼ oz)	151-proof Rum, ideally Tilambic from Mauritius

Garnish: Banana, Brown Sugar, Cinnamon (see directions below)

Prepare the banana ahead of time: Cut one slice per cocktail about 1cm (just under half an inch) thick. Sprinkle on a little brown sugar, or (better) Muscovado sugar, and cover. This can be left for up to an hour before use. If you leave it much longer than that, the banana will get mushy. When you are ready, combine all of the ingredients except the 151-proof rum in a shaker with ice cubes to have standing by ready. Do not shake it yet. Transfer one of the banana slices to the center well of a chilled Margarita glass with a metal skewer through it, resting diagonally on the side of the glass. Add the 151-proof rum and ignite. Let the fire grow for a few seconds. Sprinkle ground cinnamon into the flame for both effect and flavor. After a few seconds, shake the cocktail with the ice and strain it into the glass to extinguish the flame.

SWAYING PALMS

This cocktail goes down so smoothly that you might find yourself doing some swaying, too. The star ingredient is the very unusual Compañero rum from Panama. After aging for 12 years in oak barrels, the rum is removed and cacao beans are roasted in the same barrels. Then the rum is put back into those barrels for another 9 months. The chocolate infusion can be overwhelimg without other mitigating flavors, which is what this cocktail is all about. A big part of the delicate balance is the gentian root.

30ml (1 oz)	Rum, Compañero Panama *Extra Añejo*
22.5ml (¾ oz)	Dark Rum, Diplomático *Reserva Exclusiva*
15ml (½ oz)	Banana Liqueur, Tempus Fugit
45ml (1½ oz)	Pineapple Juice
7.5ml (¼ oz)	Lime Juice
7.5ml (¼ oz)	Grapefruit Juice
7.5ml (¼ oz)	Suze Gentian Liqueur or Amaro di Angostura
1 teaspoon	*Subtle Sweetness Liqueur
1 teaspoon	Overproof Rum, Plantation OFTD

Garnishes: Orchid, Pineapple segments on a skewer

Shake gently with ice, rocking the shaker back and forth— swaying, if you will. Then dump the contents into a fresh large coconut shell or a chilled rocks glass. Add in the garnishes and a straw.

REVIEW

"A masterpiece! The clever balance of that chocolatey rum with all of the other ingredients Is exactly what a Tiki cocktail should be: A vacation where you forget where you are at, and everything else with every sip you take. In a perfect world I would have two or three of these every night!" – Brendon Michaels

ISLAND CHARISMA

This is adaptable to any strong dark rum, or agricole rhum. It was developed with 1731 Fine & Rare 8 Year Old, but Opthimus OportO 25 Year was found to be excellent. Each rum produces somewhat different results, naturally. Kewra Extract is available in some Asian food stores and online. If you can't get it, you can substitute Orange Blossom Water, but it won't be quite the same.

45ml (1½ oz)	Dark Rum (see text above)
15g (½ oz)	Papaya Purée (see recipe below)
15ml (½ oz)	Lime Juice
15ml (½ oz)	*Charisma Cordial
½ teaspoon	Anisette Liqueur, Marie Brizard
4-5 drops	Kewra Extract (Pandarus)

Garnishes: Lime Wheel and an Edible Flower

Combine all ingredients except the Kewra. Shake hard with a lot of ice, then dump into a chilled brandy snifter. Drop the Kewra extract on top, add a lime wheel, a flower and a straw.

PAPAYA PURÉE

Weigh freshly peeled ripe papaya flesh. Add 80% of the weight in sugar and 25% (by weight) of lemon juice (*e.g.* for 100g papaya add 80g sugar and 25g lemon). Blend until smooth. Rub it through a sieve. Refrigerate!

MANGO CHARISMA

As a variation of the Island Charisma (recipe above), substitute mango purée (page 97) for the papaya purée and use a strong Jamaican rum such as Mezan *XO*, or even Smith & Cross in place of the Barbados rum.

CALDERA

This recipe was created based on Rum Nation's 121-proof Cask Strength 7 Year Réunion Rhum (not to be confused with the non-cask strength). It is more intense than a Zombie, and made for those who enjoy the fire of high octane drinks. You can't quell the fire of this beast with less alcohol. It positively needs a potent rhum.

60ml (2 oz)	Réunion Rhum (see text above)
30ml (1 oz)	Orange Juice
22.5ml (¾ oz)	Lime Juice
7.5ml (¼ oz)	Galliano Vanilla
7.5ml (¼ oz)	Grand Marnier
7.5ml (¼ oz)	Bigallet China China
7.5ml (¼ oz)	Honey Syrup (equal parts honey and water)
7.5ml (¼ oz)	*The Other* Grenadine

Garnishes: Sprig of Spearmint

Combine all ingredients and shake with ice cubes. Strain into a chilled Tiki mug with crushed ice. Add the spearmint and a straw.

ABOUT RÉUNION

Like Martinique, this is a French colony. It is a very small island just 63 kilometers (39 miles) long, yet home to nearly a million people. It lies east of Madagascar and southwest of Mauritius. Réunion has a very active volcano and three large calderas, which are gigantic sinkholes formed when the ground above a magma chamber collapses. The word *caldera* is Spanish for cooking pot. The economy is based on sugarcane and tourism, with rhum more recently adding an growing contribution, just as it has on nearby Madagascar and Mauritius. When you buy the excellent rhum from these islands, you help impoverished people.

FERIADO

The name means holiday or shoreleave in Portuguese. Some have nicknamed this a "Reverse Fogcutter" (a Fogcutter being a rum cocktail with a float of sherry), but it is really quite different.

60ml (2 oz)	Madeira, Blandy's *5 Year Reserva*
15ml (½ oz)	Apricot Liqueur, Merlet
15ml (½ oz)	Bigallet China China
15ml (½ oz)	Lemon Juice
2 dashes	Angostura Bitters
7.5ml (¼ oz)	Overproof Rum, Plantation OFTD

Do not substitute the Madeira! *Combine all of the ingredients except the overproof rum. Shake with ice and strain into a Tiki mug with ice cubes in it. Float the overproof rum.*

Y

TO PARTS UNKNOWN

This predates Bourdain's show. The liquid coats your tongue and then melts away into uncharted realms of sweet citrus groves.

50ml (1¾ oz)	Light Rum, ideally Havana Club 3
15ml (½ oz)	Dark Rum, ideally Havana Club 7
22.5ml (¾ oz)	*Charisma Cordial
15ml (½ oz)	*Golden Lime Cordial
15ml (½ oz)	Bigallet China China
15ml (½ oz)	Lime Juice
Garnish: Orange Peel (deep cut with a knife)	

Shake well with ice cubes. Dump contents into a chilled rocks glass. Spritz the orange peel over the top. Add a straw.

HAVANA GOOD TIME
(A MODERN CUBAN MAI TAI)

This has a lot in common with the classic Mai Tai (see next recipe), but sufficiently different to be worth trying for yourself. The Elixir de Cuba is banned in the U.S., but available everywhere else. Giffard's Orgeat may be substituted for the homemade version, but in that case increase the lime juice to 22.5ml (¾ oz).

45ml (1½ oz)	Ron Mulata 15 Year Rum
30ml (1 oz)	Legendario Elixir de Cuba
7.5ml (¼ oz)	Overproof Rum, Plantation OFTD
15ml (½ oz)	*Old Fashioned Orgeat (see text above)
15ml (½ oz)	Lime Juice

Garnishes: Lime Shell and Mint Sprig

Squeeze 15ml (½ oz) of half a lime's juice through a sieve into a shaker. If you can't get that much juice from half of a lime, then you need better limes, but for now add the juice from another lime, as needed. Reserve a lime shell. Add the other ingredients and shake with ice cubes. Dump all into a chilled rocks glass. Add the lime shell, the mint sprig and a straw.

🍸

The Mai Tai and Wray & Nephew 17 Year Rum

The quintessential Tiki-est of all Tiki cocktails and the Holy Grail of all cocktails because there has never been a published recipe that is 100% accurate. None of the ingredients are available in the same way they were in the 1940's, most especially the legendary 17 Year Wray & Nephew Rum. Except that Trader Vic was not using that stuff straight out of the bottle. Perhaps originally, but not by the late 1940's. If you read my previous book, *Cocktails of the*

South Pacific, then you already know my family history with Vic. One day before I was even born, Vic gave my father a half bottle of the *actual* rum he was using for the Mai Tai. It was the doctored 17 Year Wray & Nephew blended by Vic himself. My father didn't care for the Mai Tai (!) and so the bottle lingered in our cocktail cabinet for decades. I want to dispell two rumors. First, it was not 77% alcohol as some have imagined. It was about 42% (measured with a hygrometer). Also, it is important to know that all rums varied quite a lot from batch to batch back then. There was some other detective work done over the years, as well as my own unique experience in seeing Vic's secret locker with the hibiscus, vanilla and raisin infusion used. I copied the taste of my precious sample many times over the years until I finally ran out of the original and was copying a copy, I must admit. However, I stand by this recipe as the best you will ever find of what Vic ACTUALLY used. The recipe has to be altered to use currently available products.

40ml	J.M. Rhum, Martinique *XO*
40ml	Smith & Cross Rum
15ml	White Rum, Plantation 3-Star
10ml	Plantation OFTD Rum (69% ABV)
5ml	Trois Riveres Martinique Agricole Blanc Rhum
5ml	Grand Marnier
5ml	*Vic's Nastoyka

THE MAI TAI

60ml (2 oz)	17 Year Wray & Nephew Rum copy
22.5ml (¾ oz)	Cointreau
15ml (½ oz)	Orgeat, Giffard
20ml (0.7 oz)	Lime Juice

Garnishes: Two Lime Shells and a Mint Sprig

I know this is not the standard recipe. Just trust me! Shake all ingredients with ice. Dump contents into an Old Fashioned glass. Add two lime shells, the mint and a straw.

COCKTAILS THAT BEAR

REPEATING

These are either versions of classics, or forgotten drinks that have been resurrected using modern ingredients.

Y

QUEEN CONSORT

This specific cocktail is rarely seen today, but it is one of many variations of popular Madeira and Port based cocktails of the 19th Century. My guess is that the queen consort for which it was named was Queen Amalia of Spain, who was quite a character. She refused to have sex with her husband, King Ferdinand VII (who was about 20 years older than her), protesting that it would be a violation of Catholic morality for spouses to have sex with each other. It took a letter directly from the Pope to make her give in.

A sweeter and more interesting dessert drink is made with **Macadamia Nut Rum** (page 198) replacing the brandy.

60ml (2 oz)	Madeira, Blandy's *5 Year Reserva*
15ml (½ oz)	Spanish Brandy, Torres 10 (see text above)
1 teaspoon	D.O.M. Benedictine
1 whole	Lime, ribbons of peel cut with a zester
Garnish: Grated Nutmeg	

Combine all ingredients. Note that traditionally sometimes a little sugar was added, too. The macademia nut rum has plenty of sugar already, if you are using that. Shake briefly with ice cubes, then double-strain into a chilled goblet. Grate fresh nutmeg on top.

COSMIC-POLITAN

Low in alcohol, but that information is on a need-to-know basis.

15ml (½ oz)	Jägermeister
15ml (½ oz)	*Bramble Liqueur
15ml (½ oz)	Crème de Cassis, or Crème de Mure
60ml (2 oz)	Cranberry Juice, Ocean Spray

Garnish: Flamed Orange Peel

Shake with ice and strain into a chilled martini or coupe glass. Flame an orange peel over the top, then drop the peel in.

Y

ALMOST OLD FASHIONED

The combination of the Earth Tones with the cognac *almost* gives the illusion of a bourbon Old Fashioned, only more intriguing.

60ml (2 oz)	Cognac, Hennessy *VSOP*
22.5ml (¾ oz)	*Earth Tones Cordial
2 teaspoons	*The Other* Orange Liqueur
2 teaspoons	Lime Juice
1 dash	Angostura Bitters
1 dash	Orange Bitters, Angostura brand

Garnish: Orange Peel

Stir with ice and strain into a chilled rocks glass with a single large ice cube. Rub the peel over the rim, then drop it in.

Y

MONTEREY MARGARITA

A surprisingly different take on a Margarita due to the Monterey Liqueur and Golden Lime Cordial (the latter of which makes a fine addition to any Margarita).

60ml (2 oz)	Tequila, silver or reposada as you like
30ml (1 oz)	*Monterey Liqueur
30ml (1 oz)	Cointreau
30ml (1 oz)	Lime Juice
1 teaspoon	*Golden Lime Cordial
1 teaspoon	Grand Marnier

Garnishes: Lime Wedge

Salt the rim of a coupe glass for straight up, or a Margarita glass for serving on the rocks. Combine all ingredients except the Grand Marnier. Shake with ice and strain into the chilled glass. Float the Grand Marnier. Add the lime wedge on the rim.

Y

ORANGE MARGARITA

This is a great example of how *The Other* Orange Liqueur can be the suprisingly different choice over Cointreau.

50ml (1.75 oz)	Tequila, blanco (silver)
30ml (1 oz)	*The Other* Orange Liqueur
15ml (½ oz)	Lime Juice

Garnish: Orange Wedge

Combine all ingredients. Shake with ice. I suggest serving this straight up in a chilled martini glass, but on the rocks is also fine for a weaker drink.

MARJOJA-RITA

Marjoja (pronounced *mah-ree-yo-yah*) means berries in Finnish, and this is a Margarita with a Scandinavian twist. Your choice of tequila will determine if this is a casual cocktail or a smooth slow sipping powerhouse.

45ml (1 ½ oz)	Tequila, silver, reposado or añejo
22.5ml (¾ oz)	*Royal Scandinavian Cordial
15ml (½ oz)	Orange Juice
15ml (½ oz)	Lime Juice
dash	Mole Bitters, Bittermans
1 teaspoon	Grand Marnier

Garnishes: Lime Curl, Skewer of Lingonberries or Raspberries

Salt the rim of a Coupe glass for straight up, or of a Margarita glass for serving it on the rocks. Combine all ingredients except the Grand Marnier. Shake with ice and strain into the chilled glass (with or without ice in it). Float the Grand Marnier. Garnish with the skewer of berries and a lime curl.

🍸

ORANGE DAIQUIRI

What makes this special is your homemade orange liqueur.

60ml (2 oz)	Light Rum, preferably Havana Club 3 Años
30ml (1 oz)	*The Other* Orange Liqueur
15ml (½ oz)	Lime Juice

Garnish: Orange Wedge

Shake all ingredients with ice then dump the contents into a chilled glass. Add the orange to the rim and add a straw.

BOURBON PEACH SMASH

A regular summer cocktail in some parts of the southern United States for more than a century, but seldom seen in most of the rest of the world. The Tulip Cup Cordial adds complexity and spice.

60ml (2 oz)	Bourbon, Jim Beam or Jack Daniels
22.5ml (¾ oz)	Peach Liqueur or Peachtree Schnapps
15ml (½ oz)	*Tulip Cup Cordial
1 teaspoon	Lemon Juice
30ml (1 oz)	Soda Water, Fever Tree

Garnishes: Mint and slices of fresh Peach

The peach slices should be macerated in powdered sugar and bourbon several hours ahead of time. Combine all ingredients except the peach slices and the soda water. Shake with ice. Strain into a chilled rocks glass half filled with ice cubes. Add the peach slices and then more ice. Add the soda water. Garnish with mint (or spearmint). Finally, a straw.

Y

NOUVELLE SAZERAC

Embrace change. That's all I have to say about this one.

60ml (2 oz)	Cognac
15ml (½ oz)	*Sicilian Bitter Lemon Cordial
½ teaspoon	Gammel Dansk
3 dashes	Peychaud's or Boker's Bitters

Also: Absinthe, Lemon Peel

Rinse a chilled Old Fashioned glass with Absinthe. Combine all ingredients. Stir with ice then strain into the glass. Place a strip of lemon peel across the top. Wait for applause.

HOLLYWOOD BOULEVARDIER

They said it couldn't be done. Or maybe they meant it *shouldn't* be done. Either way, this is a peculiar take on the classic whiskey version of a Negroni in which the vermouth has been redesigned.

45ml (1½ oz)	Rye Whiskey, Jim Beam
30ml (1 oz)	Campari
30ml (1 oz)	Port Wine, Ruby
7.5ml (¼ oz)	Amaro Montenegro
7.5ml (¼ oz)	*Bitter Cherry Cordial
Garnish: Orange Peel	

Combine all ingredients in a mixing glass with ice cubes. Stir well. Strain into a chilled Old Fashioned glass with a single large ice cube. Add the orange peel garnish.

ITALIAN MOJITO

Back in 2012, this won first place for me in a cocktail contest in Saint Petersburg, Russia. The only difference was the Bramble Liqueur was just a mix of cranberry syrup and vodka back then.

30ml (1 oz)	Light Rum, Plantation 3-Star
30ml (1 oz)	Gin, Beefeater
22.5ml (¾ oz)	*Bramble Liqueur
22.5ml (¾ oz)	Lime Juice, fresh
6-8 whole	Basil Leaves, fresh

Muddle the basil leaves with the Bramble Liqueur very well. Add all of the other ingredients and stir with ice. Dump into a Highball glass containing more ice. Add a straw and a sprig of basil as garnish.

RAGAZZA

The full name is *Ragazza Che Prega*, which is Italian for *girl praying*. This is in reference to its cousin, the Maiden's Prayer.

45ml (1½ oz)	Gin, preferably Hendrick's
22.5ml (¾ oz)	*The Other* Orange Liqueur
22.5ml (¾ oz)	Blood Orange Juice, fresh
7.5ml (¼ oz)	Amaretto DiSaronno
7.5ml (¼ oz)	Lemon Juice
¼ teaspoon	Orange Blossom Water

Garnishes: Grapefruit Zest and edible Orange Blossom

Combine all ingredients. Stir with ice cubes for 30 seconds. Strain into either a chilled coupe glass to serve straight up, or into a chilled wine glass with crushed ice and a straw for those who prefer weaker cocktails. Rub the rim with the grapefruit peel, then discard it. Add the edible flower, if you have one.

Y

FRENCH COWBOY

A cousin of the old Drugstore Cowboy. Layer upon layer of flavor!

45ml (1 ½ oz)	Calvados
30ml (1 oz)	Grand Marnier
22.5ml (¾ oz)	*Spiced Date Syrup
22.5ml (¾ oz)	Lemon Juice
1 teaspoon	Dark Crème de Cacao, Tempus Fugit
2 dashes	Angostura Bitters

Garnish: Orange Peel

Shake with ice. Strain into a chilled rocks glass with a large ice cube. Spritz the orange peel over the top, then drop it in.

CHARM ROYALE

This was inspired by the simple Kir Royale cocktail of champagne and Crème de Cassis. Adding vodka and bitters is fairly common in Russia. I just took this a couple of steps further.

22.5ml (¾ oz)	Vodka
22.5ml (¾ oz)	Crème de Cassis
15ml (½ oz)	Sweet Italian Vermouth
15ml (½ oz)	Pineapple Juice
15ml (½ oz)	*Bramble Liqueur
7.5ml (¼ oz)	Lemon Juice
4 dashes	Orange Bitters, Angostura brand
(to taste)	Champagne (see directions below)

Prepare the base of about 100ml (3.5 oz) by combining all ingredients except the champagne. Then pass this through the finest mesh of a tamis to remove any bits of pith from the juices. Do not add ice! Store bottled in the refrigerator to get it cold. This is enough for several champagne cocktails, but the amount you use will be up to you. I suggest 15% by volume, but your own personal taste will best determine the ratio.

GIN ROYALE

As a variation, combine 30ml (1 oz) of the Charm Royale formula above (minus the champagne), 60ml (2 oz) of gin, 1 teaspoon of Cointreau and ¾ teaspoon Suze Gentian Liqueur. Stir with ice and strain over a single large ice cube in a chilled rocks glass, or for a milder cocktail, over ice cubes (in which case, add a straw). Your choice of gin is important, with Beefeater a well balanced starting point and Kyrö Napue being *very* much about the Kyrö Napue.

Y

SWAMPWATER KIWI

Much like the Charm Royale recipe on the previous page, this one began life as a simple cocktail in the 1960's: *Swampwater*, being just a mix of pineapple juice and Green Chartreuse. It was invented as marketing tool for Chartreuse at the time (see vintage ad below), as 2-component recipes often are. I always found the original to be harsh. Mellowing it out without completely destroying the concept of the pineapple and Chartreuse took a great many experiments over a period of many years. I kept coming back to the idea, searching for some flavor that could harmonize the brute strength of Green Chartreuse. The key was kiwi.

30ml (1 oz)	Green Chartreuse Liqueur
30ml (1 oz)	Kiwi Liqueur, Marie Brizard
22.5ml (¾ oz)	Light Rum, Plantation 3-Star
15ml (½ oz)	Sweet Italian Vermouth, Tosti
15ml (½ oz)	Pineapple Juice
7.5ml (¼ oz)	Lime Juice

Combine all ingredients. Shake with ice cubes and then either dump the contents into a double Old Fashioned glass, or for a milder summer cocktail, strain over crushed ice in a tall Collins glass. Either way add a straw. While not necessary, a purple orchid makes a beautiful contrast and brings out the green of the Chartreuse. A lime wheel, as shown in the ad here, is also nice.

PIS ON THE BEACH

A variation of the popular Sex on the Beach made with Pisco instead of vodka as well as a couple of other modifications.

45ml (1½ oz)	Pisco
45ml (1½ oz)	*Quality Lingonberry Juice
45ml (1½ oz)	Orange Juice
22.5ml (¾ oz)	Peach Liqueur, Giffard
1 teaspoon	Grand Marnier

Garnish: Orange Slice

Fill a Highball glass with ice cubes. Add of the ingredients except the lingonberry juice. Stir with a bar spoon. Layer the lingonberry juice. Add a straw and the garnish.

🍸

AVIATIOR

A flashback to a cocktail served in Playboy Clubs back in the late 1960's based on the Aviation. This version is more in keeping with modern tastes. Note it is a small pour for a smaller size glass.

45ml (1½ oz)	Gin, ideally Bombay Sapphire
7.5ml (¼ oz)	Parfait Amour, Bols
7.5ml (¼ oz)	*Royal Scandinavian Cordial
15ml (½ oz)	Lemon Juice, strained
1 teaspoon	Maraschino Liqueur

Garnish: Brandied Cherry, Lavender Sugar (see text below)

Rim the glass with a little Lavender Sugar (page 203). Stir ingredients with ice cubes. Strain into a small chilled Martini or Coupe glass. Add the cherry on a metal skewer.

MILLION DOLLAR COCKTAIL

This is not a modern interpretation, but rather a return to the largely forgotten original. The Million Dollar Cocktail dates back to the 1820's. These days it is usually made with gin, but genever was used at the time. It also included an infusion of local herbs in high-proof grain alcohol, so Chartreuse has been included in this recipe.

45ml (1½ oz)	Genever, ideally Bokma Oude Friesche
60ml (2 oz)	Pineapple Juice
15ml (½ oz)	Heering Cherry Liqueur
7.5ml (¼ oz)	Green Chartreuse
1 Medium	Egg White

Combine all ingredients with ice and shake vigorously for 20-30 seconds. Double strain into a chilled Nick & Nora glass.

Y

MODERN SHERRY COBBLER

Back in the early 19th Century, sherry was regarded as one of the finest spirits available. The most popular cocktail involved adding sugar and fruit to a dry type of sherry. It was served with ice and pieces of fruit floating in it, especially berries and oranges slices.

90ml (3¼ oz)	Dry Sherry, Oloroso *Seco* or Amontillado
15ml (½ oz)	Strawberry Liqueur, Bols
7.5ml (¼ oz)	Cointreau
1 teaspoon	Peach Liqueur, Giffard
½ teaspoon	Maraschino Liqueur
1 dash	Seville Orange Bitters, Scrappy's

Stir with ice and then strain into a chilled white wine glass either with or without cracked ice, as you like.

KNICKERBOCKER #3

One of the most important figures in 19th century mixology was Jerry Thomas. Many of his recipes were published in books, but it is well known that there were variations that were never published. This is a slight modification of a cross between two of his Knickerbocker cocktails. Originally the recipe called for shaking with a lemon or lime shell, but the **SUPERCHARGING** method is far superior (see my previous book, *Cocktails of the South Pacific*, for a full explanation and the history). If you want to crank this cocktail up to 11, then substitute a more potent rum in place of the light rum. I suggest Rum Nation Réunion *Cask Strength* for the brave.

45ml (1½ oz)	Madeira
45ml (1½ oz)	Light Rum, Plantation 3-Star (see text above)
2 teaspoons	Raspberry Syrup, Monin
7.5ml (¼ oz)	Lemon Juice, strained
¼ teaspoon	Orange Zest, grated
¼ teaspoon	Lime Zest, grated

Grate the orange and lime zests onto a metal sieve. Pour the rum over them, collecting the liquid in a shaker. Press down on the zests to express as much of the oil as possible, then discard the solids. Add the rest of the ingredients. Now add crushed ice and stir to cool the mixture. Double strain into a chilled Coupe glass, or serve in a rocks glass with ice cubes and a straw.

ABOUT THE NAME *KNICKERBOCKER*

This curious name means *toy marble maker* in German. It was the pen name of Washington Irving when he wrote, "The History of New York" in 1809. The Knickerbocker Hotel in New York was famous for having the richest clients, and one of the most famous cocktail bar scenes in the world...up until Prohibition, of course.

Y

MODERN PORTO FLIP

Just as Sherry and Madeira were all the rage in the 19th century, so were Port wine cocktails, though most often as an ingredient in punch bowls loaded with fruit. This is an amalgamation of recipes from the period with the pizzazz of some modern elements. Know that the egg yolk taste is loud and clear, which some people dislike.

45ml (1½ oz)	Ruby Port, Churchill's Reserve
22.5ml (¾ oz)	Cognac, Hennessy *VS* or *VSOP*
1 whole	Egg Yolk
1 teaspoon	*Falernum or substitute JDT Velvet Falernum
1 teaspoon	Lime Juice
1 teaspoon	Crème de Violette or substitute Parfait Amour
2 dashes	Angostura bitters
1 dash	Plantation OFTD Rum

Combine all ingredients and shake vigorously. Double strain into an antique crystal stemmed cocktail glass. You can use a Coupe glass if that's what you have.

DUALING GIMLETS

Mix one of these up and another using Rose's Lime Cordial in the traditional ratio. Let them fight it out, one sip at a time.

85ml (3 oz)	Gin, Tanqueray
30ml (1 oz)	*Duality Cordial
22.5ml (¾ oz)	Lime Juice, strained
Garnish: Lime Wheel	

Combine all ingredients. Stir with ice. Strain into a chilled Coupe glass. Put the lime wheel on the rim.

FRENCH TICKLER 75

The French 75 was the most popular cocktail among Russian nobility and later, of Communist Party leaders. Here it's been modfied to be more complex and in keeping with modern tastes.

60ml (2 oz)	Champagne or Crémant (which was used)
30ml (1 oz)	Gin, Bombay Sapphire
7.5ml (¼ oz)	Lemon Juice, strained
7.5ml (¼ oz)	*The Other* Grenadine
1 teaspoon	Galliano L'Autentico

Combine all of the ingredients except the champagne. Stir with ice and then strain into a chilled Martini glass. Add the champagne. A lemon curl is not traditional, but a nice touch.

Y

POST MODERN BRONX

The Bronx cocktail has enjoyed huge popularity for decades. This version is deeper, richer and more complex—bar tested and patron approved. This is an example of how a bar can attract loyal fans.

50ml (1¾ oz)	Gin, ideally Tanqueray No. Ten
22.5ml (¾ oz)	Punt E Mes
15ml (½ oz)	Dry Vermouth, Dolin
22.5ml (¾ oz)	Orange Juice, fresh and strained
7.5ml (¼ oz)	*The Other* Orange Liqueur or Grand Marnier
Garnish: Orange Peel	

Combine all ingredients. Shake with ice. Double strain into a chilled Coupe glass. Add the orange peel garnish in the usual manner, expressing the oils over the finished cocktail.

COCKTAILS WITH A STORY

A collection of recipes with some personal favorite tales and historical footnotes collected over my years in the business.

A cocktail can provide a glimpse into a long forgotten era, or just serve as a platform for the recalling of an interesting anecdote to amuse customers at the bar. Having been in the coveted position of working in Hollywood for many years with people in film and television (most now relics of the past, though) I accumulated quite a few tales that are intimately associated with particular drinks.

Some cocktails also have a historical significance. Explaining that to customers at the bar is a good ice breaker to get people talking among each other, furthering their enjoyment of the experience of the joint. A great bartender should be more than a drink making machine. They should be someone who is one part comedian, one part historian and one part psychologist. Sometimes one part confidant, too, because a bartender hears many secrets when liquor has loosened the tongue. But a good bartender is an entertainer first and foremost. To remain fresh for repeat customers, one needs to have new interesting stories to tell. My father supplied many such tales to Trader Vic back in the 1940's, who made those stories his own with embellisments galore. I chronicled that history in my previous cocktail book, for those interested. Here I've kept things fresh by selecting previously untold tales which I hope will be of interest to many. So sit down and pull up a cocktail ...or four.

Y

OLD TOM SHARP

This is a smallish cocktail, but do not attempt to make it a double by adding more gin or you will destroy the balance. The history of Old Tom Sharp and how his actions led to the death of Joseph Smith, the founder of the Mormon church, is a tale seldom heard these days. While Smith was in jail awaiting trial for the attempted murder of three men, a mob of about two hundred showed up. The jailer became nervous and warned Smith about the crowd outside before running off, but Smith had assured him that he would be just fine because those were his loyal followers who had came to rescue him. Suffice it to say, they were not.

60ml (2 oz)	Old Tom Gin, Makar (see notes below)
2 teaspoons	*Old Fashioned Orgeat
7.5ml (¼ oz)	Drambuie
7.5ml (¼ oz)	Lemon Juice
1 teaspoon	Sherry, Medium Oloroso
2 dashes	Boker's Bitters
Garnish: Lemon Zest Curl	

Combine all ingredients with ice cubes. Stir for 30 seconds, then strain into a chilled vintage sherry glass. Add the garnish.

SUBSTITUTIONS

Maker Old Tom Gin: Makar is a Scottish Old Tom gin with a unique flavor profile. As a substitute, combine 40ml (1.4 oz) of Hendrick's Gin (which is also Scottish), 15ml (½ oz) of an Oude Genever and 7.5ml (1/4 oz) Subtle Sweetness Liqueur. The volume will be half a teaspoon greater, but you can ignore that.

Boker's Bitters: Fee Bros. Cardamom Bitters will work, though not quite as well.

Y

FRUIT LOOPS

I became friends with Margaux Hemingway, the granddaughter of Ernest Hemingway, back in the 1980's. We met in a liquor store. I had just plucked up the last bottle of Taittinger *Comtes de Rosé* champagne when she let out a sigh and said how that was her favorite. Then I plucked up the courage to suggest that we share it. She agreed! Later she told me that Ernest had said that you are not an alcoholic as long as you don't drink before 11:00 in the morning. I said that's why I never get up before 10:00. So she asked why I didn't just sleep in until 11:00? I explained jokingly, "Because I can't find a wine that pairs well with Froot Loops." This little *tête-à-tête* stuck in my head. I began to ponder if such a cocktail could be built that had the flavors of that cereal but was still an "adult beverage".

60ml (2 oz)	Light Rum, Plantation 3-Star
45ml (1½ oz)	Grapefruit Juice, fresh
45ml (1½ oz)	Pineapple Juice
2 teaspoons	*The Other* Grenadine
7.5ml (¼ oz)	Cointreau
7.5ml (¼ oz)	Crème de Noyaux, Tempus Fugit
7.5ml (¼ oz)	*Falernum
7.5ml (¼ oz)	Banana Liqueur, Bols (see note below)
5-6 drops	Vanilla Extract

Garnishes: Thin slices of banana and strawberry.

Note that Tempus Fugit's banana liqueur did not exist at the time, and Bols actually works better in this recipe. Also, originally the grenadine was a bit less and Monin's was used. You can do the same, but it has more complexity with this grenadine version.

Half fill a Collins glass with ice, then add a few slices of banana and strawberry (optional). Add more ice cubes. Combine all ingredients. Shake with ice, then strain into the glass. Add a straw.

Y

MEDICINE SHOW

Many moons ago I was among the stars in the film industry. One night I made a friend who was a sound editor at Paramount over our mutual enthusiasm for cocktails, especially Tiki drinks. On several occasions I would bring in a box with some small bottles of cocktails I'd been working on, and he kept a secret stash of liquors in a locked filing cabinet. The ice came from a little cafe on the studio lot. One day a security guard looked in on us and asked what we were doing with all these little bottles. My friend told him I was a doctor. I started to correct him, but he went on to say that I was an expert in herbal remedies and he had been having problems with his breathing. That seemed to satisfy the guard, and he ducked back out while we had a laugh at his gullibility, never expecting to see him again. One of the cocktails I was testing out was this one, only without the last two ingredients. It was balanced okay, but lacked a defining character, or for lack of a better word, punch. My friend suggested adding Absinthe to it, and proceeded to do so. Now that was all you could taste, and it was all punch and no finesse. I set it aside and moved on to other things. A little while later the same security guard came back and said that one of the actors has a stuffed up head and "being a doctor", he wanted to know if I had anything to offer. My friend promptly handed him the bottle with this failed cocktail and exclaimed, "Here! This will clear *anyone's* sinuses!" He took it and walked off. A moment later I decided we should follow him because it would be funny to see the person's reaction when they get a taste of that stuff. So we walked across the compound, and low and behold the recipient was Gillian Anderson, best known as Agent Scully in the old X-Files television series. The guard gave her it and said it was from the studio doctor! She unscrewed the lid and drank the whole thing down in one gulp! We were already laughing, expecting she might scream next. Instead she calmly asked, "Does this have alcohol in it?" What a badass! Obviously she was no stranger to strong drinks. Years later I found her working behind a bar at a charity event (see photo).

The cocktail was fixed later with Marie Brizard's Anisette liqueur and Unicum Zwack in place of the Absinthe. It is best served on the rocks. But, if you want the full experience, serve it at room temperature with the Absinthe replacing those two ingredients. *That* version became known as *Gillian's Medicine*, but I don't recommend it for anything other than as a fraternity initiation unless you love absinthe. This version is far smoother.

60ml (2 oz)	Gin, Bombay Sapphire
15ml (½ oz)	Cognac, Hennessy *VSOP*
15ml (½ oz)	Lemon Juice, strained
7.5ml (¼ oz)	Crème de Cassis
7.5ml (¼ oz)	D.O.M. Benedictine
1 teaspoon	Anisette, Marie Brizard (see text)
1 teaspoon	Unicum Zwack

Combine all ingredients and stir. Served at room temperature originally, but stirred with ice is much preferred. Strain into a chilled crystal sherry glass.

REVIEW

"Another complex combination of ingredients (one of them new to me, the Zwack), comes together in a fascinating way. Up front the focus is on the anise profiles, the Anisette and Zwack together creating rich black licorice notes. The cognac rounds out the gin, and the lemon and Benedictine add punctuation. There's a subtle hint of raisins, perhaps the meeting place of the Zwack, cognac and Creme de Cassis? For me the Creme de Cassis itself didn't really emerge until some dilution set it, and then I found it an important presence in the lingering finish, and of course contributing to the lovely colour. Given the history, it seems perfectly fitting that this cocktail looks beautiful, and has a presence at once strong and mysterious." – Michael Bentley

KING ALFONSO VIII

This one is really different; Unlike any other cocktail I know of. Inspired by the simpler sherry cocktail, the Alfonso VIII, from the 1930's, this is more complex and embraces the aromas and flavors of Barcelona. Historically, King Alfonso VIII was responsible for the creation of the hallmark of Spanish cuisine and nightlife: Tapas. Back in the 12th Century, while strolling the streets with a glass of sherry in hand, he asked for a small plate of food that could also be used as a cover for his sherry. The chefs of the city went to work offering him a vast array of delicious snacks on tiny plates to cover his sherry each night. This became the tradition of tapas.

75ml (2 ½ oz)	Pimentón-Infused Sherry (see below)
22.5ml (¾ oz)	Brandy, ideally Torres 10 *Double Barrel*
15ml (½ oz)	*The Other* Orange Liqueur or Grand Marnier
2 dashes	Orange Bitters, Scrappy's *Seville Orange*

Garnishes: Grapefruit Peel and Stuffed Green Olives

Add about ⅛ teaspoon of Sweet Smoked Paprika (Pimentón) to 100ml (3.5 oz) Sherry. Most Spaniards would use a Fino Sherry for this, but I much prefer a medium Oloroso. Mix and then let stand for 1-2 hours. It is essential to let it settle. Then decant the clear liquid from the top, leaving the paprika solids behind. There will be some loss, since it can't be decanted perfectly.

Combine all ingredients. Shake with ice. Strain into either a wine glass filled with ice cubes, or a rocks glass with a single large ice cube. Spritz the grapefruit peel to express the oil over the top, then rub it on the rim before dropping it into the cocktail. Serve with green olives (not in the drink), preferably stuffed with Manchego cheese. Made for tapas!

Y

LANCE LINK: SECRET BANANA

Named for the ridiculous television show from 1970, *Lancelot Link: Secret Chimp*, featured trained chimpanzees as all of the actors in a live action James Bond spoof. This must surely have been the most difficult TV series ever attempted—and surprisingly managed to last for 17 episodes. The "secret banana" of this cocktail is that it has a strong taste of banana, yet there is very little banana in it (a mere teaspoon of liqueur). The complexity that comes in layers is what justifies this massive 10-item recipe.

30ml (1 oz)	Vodka
30ml (1 oz)	*Spiced Date Liqueur
22.5ml (¾ oz)	Jägermeister
22.5ml (¾ oz)	Calvados
15ml (½ oz)	Sherry, Medium Oloroso
7.5ml (¼ oz)	Yuzu Juice
1 teaspoon	Banana Liqueur, Tempus Fugit
1 teaspoon	*Subtle Sweetness Liqueur
¼ teaspoon	Rose Water
dash	Plantation OFTD Rum

Garnish: Dehydrated Banana Chips

Combine all ingredients except the Plantation OFTD rum. Shake with ice. Strain into a Zombie glass filled with ice. Float the dash of OFTD rum, then add a straw. Serve with a few dried banana slices on a napkin alongside, if desired. Dried banana slices are available in most larger grocery stores.

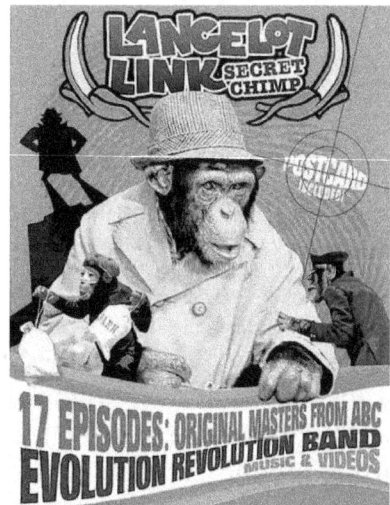

H'ANGUS THE MONKEY

Don't let this seemingly simple concoction mislead you. The balance and complexity are both excellent. Even if you hate Scotch whisky, the small amount here provides beautiful background complexity, so give it a go! Named for a truly bizarre tale about a monkey that washed ashore from a shipwreck and was mistaken for a French spy—then was executed by hanging! The fishermen who found the monkey had never seen a Frenchman and thought this might be what French people looked like! Especially because he couldn't understand a chattering word it was saying in "French". Two counties of Scotland bitterly quarrel with each other to this very day about who was to blame for this insane tragedy.

60ml (2 oz)	Vodka
22.5ml (¾ oz)	Banana Liqueur, Tempus Fugit
7.5ml (¼ oz)	Cointreau
7.5ml (¼ oz)	Lemon Juice
1 teaspoon	Scotch Whisky, Chivas Regal 12
Garnish: Lemon Peel	

Shake with ice and then strain into a lowball glass with ice cubes. Spritz lemon peel over the top. Rub the rim with it and then drop the peel in. Also add a straw.

Y

CONNECTICUT BULLFROG

The maple syrup in the original recipe for this has been swapped with a mixture of Earth Tones Cordial and Bitter Orange Cordial for complexity. One might argue that this has strayed too far from the original to be called a "version", and should be given a new name. However, if you taste the Earth Tones Cordial and Bitter Orange Cordial on their own (in the same proportions), you'll see how they work together to be like a more complex quasi-maple syrup with a strong presence of clove spice, which gives this cocktail the character that it sorely needed.

The origin of this is thought to have been a Connecticut libation known as the Windham Flip (the original detailed recipe seems to have been lost to history). In a bizarre event in the 1750's, thousands of bullfrogs descended on the town of Windham, Connecticut, due to their habibat having been destroyed in the ongoing French and Indian war. The townspeople reacted to their croaking in abject panic, thinking it was an enemy attack. Much like the tale of H'Angus the Monkey (previous page), the town became the laughing stock of everyone in neighboring areas. Rising above this, they adopted a frog as their city's symbol and even put up frog statues—and a frog on their local currency! (see photo below)

45ml (1½ oz)	Gin, Beefeater
22.5ml (¾ oz)	*Earth Tones Cordial
15ml (½ oz)	Dark Rum, Diplomático *Reserva Exclusiva*
15ml (½ oz)	Lemon Juice
½ teaspoon	*Bitter Orange Cordial

Combine all ingredients. Shake with ice and pour over crushed ice in a chilled glass. No garnish. Add a straw.

Another largely forgotten fact is that in Connecticut (up until the Civil War), there were two governors of the state elected each term, one white and one black! Since only the white male land-owning citizens were allowed to vote in the 18th century, the turnout was helped along with a party atmosphere that included free cake and free "Election Day Cocktails."

ARCHIMEDES

One of the most famous scientists of ancient times, Archimedes was born in Sicily and spent most of his life there. His most renowned tale was when he realized he had made a brilliant discovery while in the bathtub. Without dressing, he ran through the streets naked shouting, "Eureka!" in his excitement. When you taste this cocktail with Sicilian citrus and bitters, you'll say eureka! After a few, you might shout it while running down the street naked, too.

60ml (2 oz)	Rum, Zu Plun *Dolomites* Rhum (see below)
15ml (½ oz)	Averna Amaro
2 teaspoons	*Subtle Sweetness Liqueur
2 teaspoons	*Sicilian Bitter Lemon Cordial
7.5ml (¼ oz)	Lemon Juice
2 dashes	Orange Bitters, Angostura brand
15ml (½ oz)	Tonic Water, Fever Tree *Mediterranean*

Garnish: Thin spiral of lemon zest

Combine all ingredients except the tonic water. Shake with ice cubes. Strain into a chilled rocks glass containing a single large ice cube. Drop the spiral of lemon zest in.

SUBSTITUTIONS

Zu Plun *Dolomites* Rhum: This is a white Italian rum. While the sugar and molasses must be imported since the climate in Italy is not suitable for growing sugarcane, the processing, distillation and aging in barrels that were previously used for sherry and port, all take place in Italy. The flavor profile is unique and it is rather strong at 100 proof. As a substitute, I suggest a mixture of 50ml (1.75 oz) of Diplomático *Planas* Rum with 2 teaspoons of Trois Riveres Rhum *Blanc* Agricole. If this is also impossible, you can substitute another light rum, but expect less impressive results.

Y

LOLLOBRIGIDA

Named after the famous Italian actress popular in the 1950's and 1960's. This has an interesting use of saline (salt water) to modify the amaro. Bitterness has its sharpness mellowed by salt, but it only takes a very small amount to have that effect.

50ml (1.75 oz)	Gin, Tanqueray No. Ten
30ml (1 oz)	Amaro Montenegro
45ml (1 ½ oz)	Orange Juice, fresh
15ml (½ oz)	Amaretto DiSaronno
7.5ml (¼ oz)	Saline (see note below)
1 teaspoon	Maraschino Liqueur, ideally Maraska

Garnish: Spiral of Lime Zest

* **For the saline**, combine 1/4 teaspoon of table salt and 50ml (1.75 oz) of water in a jar. Shake to dissolve.

Combine all ingredients except the maraschino liqueur. Shake gently with ice. Pour contents into a Highball glass. Float the maraschino liqueur. Garnish with the lime curl and add a straw.

MORE ABOUT GINA

Gina Lollabrigida was once offered an almost unheard of six motion picture contract by Howard Hughes for a staggering sum of money, but she refused because she didn't want to leave Europe. Hughes was furious and sued every producer who hired her later, but he lost every lawsuit. Gina was promoted as being very busty, but this was before the age of plastic surgery. Her actual bust size was only 34B, but with a corset and padding she looked larger than life. Quite literally.

Y

COCOANUT GROVE COCKTAIL

The Cocoanut Grove bar was located in the Ambassador Hotel in Los Angeles. It was one of the most famous bars in the world between about 1930 and 1960. Then it began a slow decay punctuated by two especially tragic events, one being a huge fire, and then the asssassination of Robert F. Kennedy. It finally closed to guests in 1989, but was rented out as a movie set for years after.

The most famous cocktail was their signature Cocoanut Grove, which was legendary among Hollywood celebrities for decades. The funny thing is that even though the recipe was mostly printed right on the menu (here's an image from the 1930's menu)...

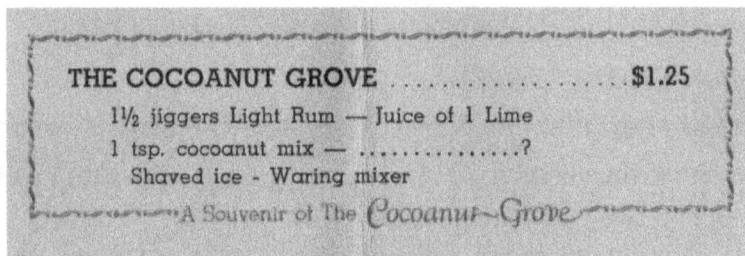

> **THE COCOANUT GROVE** $1.25
>
> 1½ jiggers Light Rum — Juice of 1 Lime
> 1 tsp. cocoanut mix — ....?
> Shaved ice - Waring mixer
>
> A Souvenir of The *Cocoanut Grove*

...yet in cocktail books the recipe is usually stated as being gin based and often containing coconut rum and grenadine, neither one of which was in it. I was in the place a couple of times before it closed. The mysterious "cocoanut mix" seemed to contain egg white, falernum and maraschino liqueur. The bartender added a tablespoon of this mix, though (not a teaspoon as stated on the menu). You can be sure this would have been made with Cuban rum originally, but you can substitute another light rum.

65ml (2 ¼ oz)	Light Rum, ideally Havana Club 3 Años
22.5ml (¾ oz)	Lime Juice
1 teaspoon	Egg White, raw (whisk to facilitate measuring)
1 teaspoon	Maraschino Liqueur
1 teaspoon	*Falernum

Combine all ingredients. Either shake vigorously with ice or blend in a mixer. Double strain into a chilled Coupe glass.

Of course the egg white, maraschino liqueur and falernum can be mixed ahead of time in a squeeze bottle for easy dispensing of a tablespoon per drink, as well as keeping the mixture a secret.

Here's the second peculiar thing about this cocktail: I don't consider it very good. Either because tastes have changed, or they were using some exquisite Cuban rum back then that is no longer available (as in the case of the Wray & Nephew 17 Year rum that was originally used in Trader Vic's famous Mai Tai).

COCOANUT GROVE COCKTAIL #2

In light of how tastes (and rums) have changed, I went to work on this cocktail at least once a month for over 20 years as a matter of habit. The recipe that I finally settled on is ironically closer to the incorrect versions published at the time in terms of the ingredients. However, the proportions are quite different. Side by side, few people today would prefer the original, but see for yourself. This is still a bit more sour compared to most cocktails these days, but less sour than most cocktails were long ago.

50ml (1¾ oz)	Gin, Beefeater
30ml (1 oz)	Lemon Juice, strained
15ml (½ oz)	Velvet Falernum, John D. Taylor's
2 teaspoons	Egg White, raw (whisk to facilitate measuring)
7.5ml (¾ oz)	Maraschino Liqueur, Maraska
1 teaspoon	Grapefruit Juice, strained

Garnish: None, or be creative.

As before, combine all ingredients. Either shake vigorously with ice of flash blend. Double strain into a chilled Coupe glass. There is no garnish for either the original or this version.

One last thing: That $1.25 cocktail on their 1935 menu converts to $25 in today's money. It was a swanky place for the wealthiest of patrons.

Y

GRETA GARBLED

Greta Garbot, the legendary *femme fatale* Swedish actress had a well known rum cocktail named after her, and she was none too happy about it because her spirit of choice was Aquavit. She tried to promote Aquavit frequently in America (see story below) but her attempts were in vain, as Aquavit never became popular in the U.S.

60ml (2 oz)	Aquavit, O.P. Anderson
15ml (½ oz)	Peach Liqueur, Giffard
15ml (½ oz)	Grapefruit Juice, strained
15ml (½ oz)	Lemon Juice, strained
1 dash	Creme de Menthe, White
Garnish: Mint Leaf	

Combine all ingredients. Stir with ice. Strain contents into a chilled Nick and Nora glass. Float one mint leaf (optional).

GARBOT IN HOLLYWOOD

Although she spent most of her time in New York City, the film industry required her to be in Hollywood frequently. My father met actor John Barrymore sometime in the late 1930's. Barrymore had been the co-star in Garbot's 1932 Academy Award winning film, *Grand Hotel*. Naturally the subject of cocktails came up, and Barrymore recalled a party in Hollywood hosted by Garbot in which Aquavit was the only drink made available to guests and everyone had to swim naked in her pool before they were allowed to leave! For many years I thought this was probably just some story made up by Barrymore, until a book published in 2018 (*Apertif* by Kate Hawkings) recounts the same story, and not from Barrymore. The cocktail named after her had nothing to do with what she drank. She preferred straight Aquavit, and this one, which was garbled by the media at the time with recipes that were completely wrong.

DAME LORRAINE

Dame Lorraine is a traditional Carnival character in Trinidad and Tobago. This cocktail is dominated by both the Amaro and the bitters from Trinidad. The idea here was to bring out the herb and spice notes in Angostura bitters that are usually concealed, dancing in the shadows. The character of Dame Lorraine goes back to the 17th Century, being a plantation owner's wife portrayed as ridiculously fat because of how much she got to eat by comparison to the their slaves. Although slavery was abolished in the 1830's there, this Carnival character lives on.

30ml (1 oz)	Spanish Brandy, Torres 10
22.5ml (¾ oz)	Rum, Diplomático *Reserva Exclusiva*
22.5ml (¾ oz)	Amaro Di Angostura
15ml (½ oz)	Grapefruit Juice, fresh
2 teaspoons	*Spiced Date Liqueur
7.5ml (¼ oz)	*Falernum
3-4 dashes	Angostura Bitters

Combine all ingredients except the Angostura bitters. Shake with ice cubes. Strain over crushed ice in a brandy snifter. Sprinkle the Angostura bitters on top of the ice. Add a straw.

🍸

DEDICATED TO MILDRED, BUT SHE WASN'T LISTENING

One night long ago, I was in a bookstore in Pasadena when an elderly woman came in with a box of old books on magic tricks to sell. The store owner offered her only a few dollars, so I said that I would pay ten times that much. She was elated and invited me to her home. Her deceased husband had been a magician long ago and she had a garage full of books, props and other interesting artifacts collected over the decades. I took on the task of selling these things for a small share of the proceeds. Within a few months I had raised nearly a hundred thousand dollars for her. One of the things she gave me in return was a half bottle of a rare 1921 French armagnac that we could not legally sell. She only drank cocktails and never straight hard liquor, and she didn't know of any cocktail recipe featuring such an armagac. Naturally, I went about inventing a cocktail that would take advantage of this amazing liquor. Unfortunately, she never had a chance to sample this spirit, now being one herself.

60ml (2 oz)	Pisco, ideally Waqar
15ml (½ oz)	*Charisma Cordial
2 teaspoons	Pimento Dram, such as The Bitter Truth
¼ teaspoon	Orange Zest, grated (see procedure below)
1 teaspoon	Armagnac, ideally finest quality (see text)

Grate the orange zest onto a sieve. Carefully pour the pisco over the top of it, pressing down on the zest to express as much of the oils as you can. Now discard the zest and add the other ingredients except for the armagnac. Stir with ice. Double strain into a chilled rocks glass with a single large ice cube. Gently float the armagnac on top. A very complex aroma and taste emerges.

REVIEW

"It's fair to say this is built around the Charisma Cordial. In the context of the of this recipe, the citrus notes of the cordial are picked out by the super-charging of the pisco with orange zest, and surprisingly well countered by the pimento dram, lending the cocktail an interesting orange and spice orientation, while still tasting very fresh. Having tried this drink with and without the Armagnac float, I can attest to how much better it is with the float; The Armagnac an important complimentary note to the allspice liqueur. Another well rendered and complex profile here, I think the spirit of Mildred would definitely approve!" — M.B.

Curiouser and Curiouser
NEW COCKTAILS
from the
TRAVELS
and IMAGINATION
of the
AUTHOR

I consider one of the most important things in cocktail design is not to fall into a habit of repeating the same flavor over and over. It is human nature and something that must be consciously avoided.

Y

WHITE RABBIT

An ambassador from Russia dined with us and requested a cocktail, specifying "*Please* not a White Russian, because I'm tired of that old joke." By chance, this one had been worked out the very night before and was waiting to be tested. He loved it and asked for the recipe, but as soon as it came to explaining how to prepare the coconut rum, he said he would just order another one. Less lime juice was used for him because Russians hate anything too sour, reminding them of spoiled food in Soviet times.

60ml (2 oz)	Gin, Tanqueray
30ml (1 oz)	*Homemade Coconut Rum
22.5ml (¾ oz)	Lime Juice (originally less)
22.5ml (¾ oz)	*Russian Milk Liqueur
7.5ml (¼ oz)	D.O.M. Benedictine
4 dashes	Elemakule Tiki Bitters, Bittermens

Combine all ingredients with ice cubes. Shake gently, then double strain the contents into a chilled Old Fashioned glass with fresh ice cubes. Add a straw.

136

DEW DROPS ON LAVENDER PETALS

The Earth Tones Cordial modifies the flavor profile of the anise liqueur, so even if you think you do not like anise flavor, try this one!

60ml (2 oz)	Gin, Beefeater
22.5ml (¾ oz)	Anisette, Marie Brizzard
22.5ml (¾ oz)	Parfait Amour, Bols
7.5ml (¼ oz)	Lemon Juice
1 dash	Angostura Bitters

Garnish: Lavender Sugar (page 203)

Rub cut lemon on the edge of a chilled Coupe or Martini glass, then roll in sugar. Do not get sugar in the bowl! Combine all ingredients and shake with ice. Double strain into the glass.

Y

ROYAL SCANDINAVIAN APERTIF

This is "high octane" example of the type of in-house secret recipe apertif served in many fine dining restaurants in Finland.

75ml (2 ½ oz)	Vodka, ideally Absolut or Finlandia
22.5ml (¾ oz)	*Royal Scandinavian Cordial
2 dashes	Grapefruit Bitters, Fee. Bros.
5-6 drops	Pernod

Garnish: Skewer of Lingonberries or Red Currants

Stir with ice. Double strain into a chilled tulip glass. This may be divided into two smaller glasses for guests. Put the skewer of berries into the drink, using a skewer long enough to be lifted out easily. Sometimes the berries are just dropped in.

GRAF ZEPPELIN COCKTAIL

In the 1930's, cocktails and fine dining aboard an airship were the *height* of luxury. This is quite complex for only a few ingredients.

60ml (2 oz)	Gin, Tanqueray
15ml (½ oz)	D.O.M. Benedictine
15ml (½ oz)	Lime Juice, fresh
2 teaspoons	*The Other* Grenadine or 1 t. ordinary grenadine
4 dashes	Orange Bitters, Angostura brand

Garnishes: Half a Strawberry and ½ teaspoon Strawberry Liqueur

Fill a chilled crystal glass just over halfway with cracked ice. Add all of the ingredients to the glass. Stir. Float the strawberry liqueur. Add a straw and the strawberry on the rim.

Y

DARTH VODKA

A fictional character who is "always late for work due to his vodka hangovers, sings karaoke in falsetto and smells like lighter fluid." To the uninitiated, Stroh 60 is reminiscent of lighter fluid. Preserved black limes can be obtained from Middle Eastern grocery stores.

60ml (2 oz)	Vodka, ideally Blavod or other black vodka
22.5ml (¾ oz)	Stroh 60 (120 proof Austrian Rum)
22.5ml (¾ oz)	*Bitter Cherry Cordial
22.5ml (¾ oz)	Cranberry Juice, Ocean Spray
2 teaspoons	*The Other* Grenadine or 1 t. ordinary grenadine

Garnish: Half of a Preserved Black Lime (see text above)

Combine all ingredients. Shake with ice cubes. Strain into a rocks glass with cracked ice. Add the black lime and a straw.

A SMILE AND A GUN

A smile can get you far, but a smile and a gun can get you further.
— Al Capone

This is a cocktail that was created for the Bathtub Gin produced by Ableforth (not to be confused with Ableforth's *Old Tom* Bathtub Gin, which is quite different). You can substitute Beefeater and still have a good cocktail, but the truly unique character shines even brighter with their Bathtub Gin. As for the Orange IV Syrup, this is even more interesting with the syrup having fermented for about 2 months (page 199). One word of caution: Some dislike anything bitter, *but* this is not nearly as bitter as a Negroni.

60ml (2 oz)	Bathtub Gin, Ableforth's (see text above)
15ml (½ oz)	*Bitter Cherry Cordial
1 teaspoon	*Bitter Orange Cordial
1 teaspoon	*Orange IV Syrup (see text above)
30ml (1 oz)	San Pellegrino Pompelmo (see note below)
Garnish: Slice of Grapefruit Peel	

* San Pellegrino Pompelmo is an Italian grapefruit soda that is widely available in grocery stores.

Combine all ingredients except the Pompelmo. Stir with ice. Strain over a single large ice cube in a chilled Old Fashioned glass. Add the Pompelmo and give it a quick stir. Garnish with a slice of grapefruit peel, rubbing it around the rim first.

ABLEFORTH'S BATHTUB GIN

Original bathtub gin in the days of Prohibition was grain alcohol infused with juniper and herbs, but not distilled. Ableforth starts out with distilled gin and then infuses it with six more herbs for a week.

♈

YUCATAN SOUR

The sourness is tempered by a gallery of bewildering flavors that dance on the palate. The aroma is almost mystical from the unique homemade kumquat liquor. Just a slight bit of heat from the chili liqueur reminds you that this isn't any ordinary tequila cocktail.

60ml (2 oz)	Reposada Tequila, Los Tonas
22.5ml (¾ oz)	*Fermented Salty Kumquat Liqueur
15ml (½ oz)	Lime Juice, strained
7.5ml (¼ oz)	*Duality Cordial
7.5ml (¼ oz)	Ancho Reyes *Verde* Poblano Chile Liqueur

Combine all ingredients. Shake gently with ice. Either dump the contents into a chilled Margarita glass or double strain into a chilled Martini glass for an even more intense experience.

Y

JAMES AND THE GIANT BITCH

Named after a customer who pestered us daily at a Tiki bar for cocktails featuring Scotch. I strongly suggest using Balvenie DoubleWood 12 Year Old for this, because it doesn't overpower the other flavors with smoke and iodine the way that Scotch often does.

60ml (2 oz)	Scotch, Balvenie DoubleWood 12 Year
22.5ml (¾ oz)	Galliano Vanilla
7.5ml (¼ oz)	*Earth Tones Cordial
7.5ml (¼ oz)	Lemon Juice
3-4 dashes	Peach Bitters, Fee Bros.

Combine all ingredients. Stir with ice and then strain into a rocks glass with a single large ice cube.

ONCE UPON A LIME

There's some Fairy Godmother magic in this one. It's based on my recollection of a cocktail prepared by my godmother long ago. I don't know what went into it, but she had some kind of witch's brew with citrus bubbling away first. It's a fairytale with a happy ending!

45ml (1½ oz)	Gin, Tanqueray No. Ten
22.5ml (¾ oz)	Mandarine Napoleon Liqueur
15ml (½ oz)	*Golden Lime Cordial
7.5ml (¼ oz)	Lime Juice, strained
1 teaspoon	*Bitter Orange Cordial
5-6 drops only	Cardamom Bitters, Fee Bros.
2-3 drops	Orange Blossom Water

Garnish: Lime Zest Strip

Stir all ingredients with ice. Double strain into a chilled Coupe glass. Wind the lime zest into a tight coil and put on rim.

🍸

BLACK FOREST CAKE VODKA

I prefer desserts that I can drink — Foster Brooks

60ml (2 oz)	Vodka
22.5ml (¾ oz)	Kirschwasser, Schwarzwälder
15ml (½ oz)	Heering Cherry Liqueur
15ml (½ oz)	Dark Crème de Cacao, Tempus Fugit
15ml (½ oz)	*Duality Cordial
7.5ml (¼ oz)	Lemon Juice, strained
2 dashes	Aztek Chocolate Bitters, Fee Bros.

Combine ingredients. Shake with ice. Double strain into a cold Coupe glass. Serve with a cube of bittersweet chocolate.

LA SCALA

Named after the famed opera house in Italy. While this might appear to be some kind of Negroni, it's sweet and quite different. A touch of cognac elevates this from a pop song to a soprano aria.

45ml (1½ oz)	Gin, Beefeater
30ml (1 oz)	Orange Juice, fresh
22.5ml (¾ oz)	*Sicilian Bitter Lemon Cordial
15ml (½ oz)	Campari
15ml (½ oz)	*The Other Orange Liqueur
7.5ml (¼ oz)	Cognac, Hennessy XO, or a fine Armagnac
Garnish: Wedge of freshly cut Orange	

Combine all ingredients except the cognac. Shake with cracked ice. Strain into a chilled rocks glass with a single large ice cube. Drop in the orange wedge and then float the cognac.

Y

THE HALLUCINOGENIC TOREADOR

Named after the painting by Dali. The combination of the sweet and dry sherry wines creates a rich and complex flavor. The ideal dry sherry for this is Alfonso Oloroso Seco by González Byass.

45ml (1½ oz)	Spanish Brandy, Torres 10 Double Barrel
15ml (½ oz)	Sherry, Seco (dry - see text above)
15ml (½ oz)	Sherry, Lustau Pedro Ximénez San Emilio
7.5ml (¼ oz)	Cointreau
7.5ml (¼ oz)	Lemon Juice, strained
1 dash	Seville Orange Bitters, Scrappy's

Shake well with ice cubes. Double strain into an antique crystal goblet or a wine glass.

BLOOD ON THE SADDLE

Named after the vintage Tex Ritter western song that has seemingly drunken off-key guitar plucking. A problem in creating bourbon cocktails is that almost anything you do winds up tasting like a version of a Manhattan because the distinctive taste of the bourbon is so strong. If you add so many other strong ingredients to overpower that, then you can't tell it is bourbon any longer, and that's also a failure. The Chambord liqueur is a replacement for the original Mesimarja Liqueur (Arctic Brambleberry), which is actually better, but nearly impossible to find outside of Finland.

60ml (2 oz)	Bourbon, ideally Eagle Rare 10 Year
15ml (½ oz)	*Red Elk Cordial
15ml (½ oz)	White Port
15ml (½ oz)	Chambord Liqueur (see note above)
15ml (½ oz)	Lemon Juice
1 teaspoon	*Bitter Orange Cordial
2 dashes	Angostura Bitters

Combine all ingredients except the Angostura Bitters. Shake with ice. Strain over a single large ice cube in a chilled Old Fashioned glass. Add the Angostura Bitters on top and give it a quick light stir. No garnish.

SALTY KUM ON THE SADDLE

As an interesting variation, replace the lemon juice with the same amount of *Fermented Salty Kumquat Liqueur. Leave out both the Chambord and the Bitter Orange Cordial. Add 15ml (½ oz) of vodka in place of those two ingredients. Float a teaspoon of cream.

Y

Fun fact: The politically correct gender-neutral term for cowboys and cowgirls is now cowpeople.

FAME

Fame is earned with blood, not tears — Margaux Hemingway

This eclectic cocktail has many fleeting moments and moods.

60ml (2 oz)	Vodka
22.5ml (¾ oz)	*Bitter Cherry Cordial
22.5ml (¾ oz)	Lemon Juice, strained
15ml (½ oz)	Aperol
15ml (½ oz)	Chambord Black Raspery Liqueur
4-5 drops	Pernod

Garnish: Sprig of Spearmint and a Grapefruit Wedge

Combine all ingredients. Shake with ice cubes. Strain into a chilled Nick and Nora glass. Slice the grapefruit rind. Tuck in the spearmint in the gap, then slide the pulp-side onto the rim.

🍸

ROMANESQUE

Derived from an ancient Roman drink. Your selection of vermouth will strongly influence the outcome. Tosti *Rosso* works fine, though.

60ml (2 oz)	Italian Sweet Vermouth (see text above)
22.5ml (¾ oz)	*Bitter Orange Cordial
15ml (½ oz)	Vodka
1 teaspoon	Chambord (see page 38 for a substitute)
1 teaspoon	*Tulip Cup Cordial
½ teaspoon	Amaretto DiSaronno
3 dashes	Seville Orange Bitters, Scrappy's

Combine everything and stir with ice. Strain into a chilled Coupe glass or gilded goblet and serve straight up.

50 CENTS FOR YOUR SOUL

Hollywood is a place where they'll pay you a thousand dollars for a kiss and fifty cents for your soul.

— Marilyn Monroe

This is a sexy little cocktail that's sure to turn heads with its unusual garnish and vanilla aroma. It has an extremely complicated taste with many waves of different notes. It commands you to order another and then another as you try to figure it out.

45ml (1½ oz)	Dark Rhum, ideally Dzama *Cuvée Noir*
30ml (1 oz)	*Monterey Liqueur
15ml (½ oz)	Lime Juice
7.5ml (¼ oz)	Sabra Liqueur (see page 45 for a substitute)
1 teaspoon	Plantation OFTD Rum
1 teaspoon	Grand Marnier
3 dashes	Seville Orange Bitters, Scrappy's

Garnish: Vanilla Bean, Lime Wheel and Luxardo Cherry

Cut a vanilla bean in half, then split one of the halves lengthwise. Use a chopstick to pierce a Luxardo cherry all the way through. Use a toothpick to pierce the center of the lime wheel. Put the vanilla bean through the cherry and then through the lime wheel. Combine all of the ingredients and shake with ice. Strain into a Highball glass with ice cubes. Set the garnish on top so the lime slice floats on the ice at the edge of the glass with the cherry and vanilla bean showing as though it was a hat. Add a straw, but not a black straw or it will blend in with the vanilla bean. Preferably a silver metal straw or a clear plastic straw.

Y

THE FAST AND THE CURIOUS

This is a sort of "be your own bartender" Margarita served with a shaker of a mysterious liquid waiting to be added to your own liking.

30ml (½ oz)	Vodka
30ml (½ oz)	*Quality Lingonberry Juice
30ml (½ oz)	Mango Purée (see page 97)
15ml (½ oz)	Lime Juice
2 teaspoons	Mezcal
2 teaspoons	Cognac, Hennessy *VSOP*
1 teaspoon	Calvados

Combine the first four ingredients. Shake with ice and strain into an iced Margarita glass. Combine the other three liquors in a syringe to present along with the cocktail. The guest squeezes in a bit at a time to find the mixture they like best.

WHAT WAITS AT THE NORTH HORIZON

The balance of this cocktail relies on the award winning Finnish gin, Napue. Judging by the red color, *what waits* is either romantic or bloody tragic. Oh, well. It's hard to have one without the other.

60ml (2 oz)	*Quality Lingonberry Juice
30ml (1 oz)	Napue Gin (do not substitute)
22.5ml (¾ oz)	*Charisma Cordial
3 dashes	Boker's Bitters
Garnish: Lingonberries or raspberries	

Shake well with ice. Double strain into a chilled Coupe glass or decorative goblet. Lay a skewer of berries across the rim.

RUDOLPH'S LAST CHANCE

This has been described as a more elaborate version of *What Waits at the North Horizon* (recipe on the previous page.) Served before roasted reindeer, the name jokes that if you drink enough of these, you might forget about the reindeer and spare old Rudolph.

45ml (1½ oz)	Napue Gin (do not substitute)
22.5ml (¾ oz)	*Royal Scandinavian Cordial
7.5ml (¼ oz)	*Quality Lingonberry Juice
7.5ml (¼ oz)	Punt E Mes
7.5ml (¼ oz)	Lemon Juice
1 teaspoon	*Sicilian Bitter Lemon Cordial
30ml (1 oz)	Seltzer Water

Garnish: Frozen Lingonberries or Raspberries, Mint

Combine all ingredients except the seltzer water. Shake with ice. Strain into a Highball glass with cracked ice. Drop frozen berries in and a sprig of mint. Add a straw.

Y

SACRILEGE

Adding anything to a fine aged armagnac is widely regarded as sacrilege. But, in blind tastings, this was unanimously regarded as improving Tariquet Hors d'Age Bas-Armagnac as well as others. The one failure was with a 1963 (50 year old) armagnac which it made worse, not surprisingly. You just can't improve on perfection.

60ml (2 oz)	Armagnac, modest quality (see text above)
7.5ml (¼ oz)	*Herbal Wonder Liqueur

Combine ingredients in a brandy snifter and swirl to combine. Serve at room temperature.

CUECA

The name is the national dance of Chile, which is where the base ingredient of this comes from. This expresses the pure flavor of Pisco, so if that's not a flavor you enjoy, this one's not for you.

45ml (1½ oz)	Pisco, ideally Waqar (from Chile)
22.5ml (¾ oz)	Lemon Juice, strained
22.5ml (¾ oz)	*The Other* Grenadine
15ml (½ oz)	Orange Juice, fresh and strained
2 teaspoons	Egg White, beaten to facilitate measuring
1 teaspoon	Gammel Dansk

Combine all ingredients. Shake vigorously with ice. Double strain over ice cubes in a double rocks glass with a straw, or straight up in a chilled Coupe glass.

Y

TRAIL BLAZER

An exciting rush of endorphins is followed by a slow winding path into nostalgia for the dusty trail of the Old West. The unusual Borgo San Daniele Santòn Agricultural Vermouth with 20 botanical herbs is a critical component of this carefully balanced recipe.

60ml (2 oz)	Rye Whiskey, ideally Millstone 100
30ml (1 oz)	Mezcal
15ml (½ oz)	Santòn Agricultural Vermouth
15ml (½ oz)	*Subtle Sweetness Liqueur
2 dashes	Orange Bitters, Angostura brand
Garnish: Orange Peel Curl	

Combine all ingredients. Shake with ice. Strain over a single large ice cube in an Old Fashioned glass. Add the orange peel.

STARDUST AND RUST

Wisdom is in looking at the future with the eyes of the past. This is a cocktail for contemplation. Is morality purely subjective?

60ml (2 oz)	Gin, Tanqueray
30ml (1 oz)	Mandarine Orange Juice, fresh
7.5ml (¼ oz)	*Apricot Cognac
7.5ml (¼ oz)	Lime Juice
7.5ml (¼ oz)	*Herbal Wonder Liqueur
1 teaspoon	Suze Gentian Liqueur
½ teaspoon	Amaretto DiSaronno

Combine all ingredients. Stir with ice and then strain over a single large ice cube in a double rocks glass.

Y

GREEN STEM

This dates back over 25 years for me, but it is still just as tantilizing, and my absolute favorite cocktail with Crème de Menthe.

45ml (1½ oz)	Gin, Beefeater
30ml (1 oz)	*Russian Milk Liqueur
15ml (½ oz)	Amaro Montenegro
7.5ml (¼ oz)	Cognac, Hennessy *VSOP*
2 teaspoons	Green Crème de Menthe, Bols
1 teaspoon	Lime Juice, strained

Chill a tall, narrow V-shaped glass, or if not available, use a champagne flute. Mix the Crème de Menthe and lime juice in the glass. Stir the other ingredients with large ice cubes so they don't break up. Carefully strain into the glass as the top layer.

BERGAMOT ORANGE GIN

When in season, the distinctive flavor of bergamot makes for an extraordinary gin cocktail. The bitters recipe is on page 204.

75ml (2½ oz)	Gin, Tanqueray
15ml (½ oz)	Bergamot Juice, fresh
7.5ml (¼ oz)	Amaro Montenegro
7.5ml (¼ oz)	*The Other* Grenadine
2 to 3 dashes	Bergamot Bitters
Splash	Tonic Water, Fever Tree *Indian*

Combine all ingredients except the tonic water and stir with ice cubes. Strain into a chilled rocks glass with a single large ice cube (preferably spherical). Add the tonic water and stir.

Y

CROIX-DES-BOUQUETS

Named after a city in Haiti with where the sun turns dark red and the sky goes orange every sunset. As mentioned before there are two categories of Haitian rum—do not use Clairin for this one.

45ml (1½ oz)	Rhum Barbancourt (see text above)
15ml (½ oz)	Apricot Brandy (not liqueur)
15ml (½ oz)	Mandarine Juice, strained
7.5ml (¼ oz)	Averna Amaro
7.5ml (¼ oz)	Lime Juice, strained
½ teaspoon	*Vic's Nastoyka
Garnish: Luxardo Cherry	

Combine all ingredients and shake with ice. Strain into a chilled Coupe glass. Add the cherry on a skewer.

CRUSHED ROSE VELVET

Pomelo juice is seldom specified as a cocktail ingredient, but the difference between pomelo and grapefruit is essential in this.

60ml (2 oz)	Dubonnet
30ml (1 oz)	Pomelo Juice, fresh
15ml (½ oz)	Sour Rhubarb Liqueur, DeKuyper
7.5ml (¼ oz)	Gin, Tanqueray No. Ten
7.5ml (¼ oz)	*Cloudy Pear Vodka or Absolut Pears Vodka
Garnish: Dried Rose	

Combine all ingredients and stir with cracked ice. Strain into a chilled Martini glass or serve on the rocks. Float a dried rose on the surface (available in Middle Eastern food stores).

Y

TRANSCENDENTAL INIBRIATION

This is certainly an intriguing cocktail, but it also serves as an etude for the ADSR envelope (page 66) because each of the phases can be tasted separately and clearly with time between.

50ml (1¾ oz)	Tanqueray No. Ten
22.5ml (¾ oz)	Lemon Juice, strained
15ml (½ oz)	Apricot Brandy (not liqueur), Bols is okay
7.5ml (¼ oz)	Cognac, Hennessy *VS* or *VSOP*
7.5ml (¼ oz)	Ginger Liqueur, Bols
7.5ml (¼ oz)	*Charisma Cordial
7.5ml (¼ oz)	Anisette, Marie Brizard
1½ dashes	Orange Bitters, Angostura brand

Combine all ingredients. Stir with ice cubes and then strain into a chilled Old Fashioned glass containing a large ice cube.

LAAVA'S GREATEST HITS

For those of you who don't know about Laava, it was a gigantic and grand restaurant / bar located in Helsinki, Finland, of which I was a part owner as well as being in charge of the menus of both the restaurant and bar operations. The extended forced closure of all restaurants, bars and hotels due to the Covid-19 pandemic finished us off, like so many other businesses.

As much as I would like to share all of the cocktail recipes here, there are two problems. First, many of them would not be appreciated much elsewhere because they contained relatively little alcohol. Up until shortly before Laava opened, Finland had a strict law against cocktails containing more than 20ml (2/3 ounce) of hard liquor. Even though that was repealed in time for Laava's opening, the fact is that Finnish people had only had such weak cocktails for generations, so many weak cocktails were included on the menu.

The other problem in making all of the dozens of cocktail recipes from Laava's bar in their original authentic form is that many relied on liquors and liqueurs that are local only to Finland and are not exported. There would be no point in including pages of recipes that call for ingredients such as an apple-licorice liqueur made by monks living in a monastery near the Arctic Circle, or a gin flavored with sea buckthorn berries that's scarce even here. There are many specialty products that I intentionally used to provide tourists with a taste of those things they would not have experienced before. When it comes to writing those recipes for people outside of Finland, it is another matter. That's why this section is relatively short compared to Laava's extensive cocktail menu.

Even so, some liberties have been take here and there to copy recipes only as much as possible using more readily available liquors that still work.

WHITE WEDDING

Second only to the Mai Tai, the White Wedding cocktail sold the most of any of Laava's alcoholic drinks (not counting beer and wine). Kyro Dairy Cream Liqueur is a Finnish product, but I have provided a recipe for a substitute on page 201. The coconut water is the same one sold in better grocery stores these days as a non-carbonated beverage under many brand names.

45ml (1½ oz)	Coconut Water
30ml (1 oz)	Kyro Dairy Cream Liqueur (see text above)
30ml (1 oz)	Light Rum, Havana Club 3 Year
2 teaspoons	White Crème de Cacao
2 teaspoons	Pernod
2 teaspoons	Amaretto DiSarono
2 dashes	Orange Bitters, Fee Bros.

Garnish: Licorice Root Powder

Combine all ingredients in a blender jar. Add 80g (2.8 oz) of ice cubes. Blend until the ice is completely incorporated and it is frothy. Pour into a chilled mug with a handle. Dust with a little licorice root powder. The garnish is two paper umbrellas made into a lantern as shown in the photo below.

At Laava this cocktail was served in a custom made white ceramic skull mug, as shown here. The title of the drink is in reference to the song by Billy Idol in which his girlfriend suddenly gets married to someone else unexpectedly.

DOCTOR KU

The libation of choice for those who want to become "heavily socialized" as the Finns often say. Originally J. Bally *Vieux Agricole Millésime 1997 Rhum* was used, but when the supply ran out we switched to Clément *XO Rhum Agricole*. Some might wonder how we could afford to pour such high quality spirits in cocktails. Simple: The price covered it. A Doctor Ku sold for a whopping 40 euros, which is nearly US $50. On a busy night we would sell many, although often customers would share the drink with others at their table because of how strong it is with 120ml (over 4 ounces) of liquor. Like the classic Zombie, there was a supposed limit of two per customer (though never actually enforced). On more than a few occasions the festivities became a bit raucous, shall we say? Doctor Ku was almost always the culprit. But that's another story.

Vana Tallinn is an Estonian liqueur that is sold in several different strengths as well as a cream version. The best is actually the 50% alcohol one, but that's nearly impossible to get outside of Estonia. The 40% is just fine in cocktails. Avoid the cream one. Vana Tallinn is described in a bit more detail on page 32.

45ml (1½ oz)	Vana Tallinn Liqueur (40% alcohol)
30ml (1 oz)	Martinique Agricole Rhum (see text above)
30ml (1 oz)	Cognac, Hennessy *VSOP*
22.5ml (¾ oz)	Lime Juice
15ml (½ oz)	Ginger Liqueur, Giffard *Ginger of the Indies*
2 dashes	Xocolatl Mole Bitters, Bittermens

Garnish: Quarter of a Lime

Combine all of the ingredients in a shaker. Add a copious amount of crushed ice. Tumble gently, then dump the contents into a chilled Tiki mug. Squeeze the quarter lime over the top and then drop it in. Add a straw.

HUBERT'S HALO

You can make this with a dark rum such as Diplomatico *Mantuano* with reasonable results, but if you want this cocktail to really shine, you need to up your game to a serious rum. My optimum choice is Rhum J.M. *Multimillésime 2002-2007-2009* from Martinique. Now you have a cocktail worthy of a halo! The orange juice should be passed through the finest mesh of a tamis twice to remove every bit of the pulp and provide a crystal clear cocktail.

45ml (1½ oz)	Dark Rum (see text above)
30ml (1 oz)	D.O.M. Benedictine
22.5ml (¾ oz)	Jägermeister
15ml (½ oz)	Orange Juice, strained (see above)
1 teaspoon	Gold Strike Liqueur
2 dashes	Grapefruit Bitters, Scrappy's
4-5 drops	Pernod

Garnish: Inscribed Mandarine Wheel (see text below)

Cut a slice of the mandarine and then use a ring mold to cut away the interior, leaving only the outer ring. This is the "halo" garnish. Combine all ingredients. Shake with ice. Place the mandarine ring in a chilled Coupe glass and strain the contents of the shaker over it. Some people nibble on the ring as they sip.

🍸

MORE ABOUT HUBERT

Hubert is the patron saint of hunters, although he gave up hunting after a religious vision of a stag (as in the Jägermeister logo) convinced him that he was headed to Hell. After his death, his bones were exhumed and moved to a Benedictine monastery (thus the Benedictine liqueur). He was especially known for having invented a treatment for rabies in which the victim was branded with a red hot nail or key. Such was religion/medicine in those days.

OMAR KHAYAM

An exotic drink that's really memorable. This one was from a 1960's San Francisco bar recipe reworked with modern liquors. Back when cocktails were served to minors with a parent present.

30ml (1 oz)	Vodka
25ml (0.9 oz)	Ginger Liqueur, Giffard *Ginger of the Indies*
22.5ml (¾ oz)	Sweet Vermouth, Antica Formula
15ml (½ oz)	Absolut Extrakt
15ml (½ oz)	Ouzo
1 dash	Seville Orange Bitters, Scrappy's
1 dash	Angostura Bitters
Garnish: Orange Peel	

Combine all of the ingredients. Shake with ice. Strain into a chilled rocks glass with a single large ice cube. Snap the orange peel to express the oils over the drink, then drop in the peel.

Y

KIVA VERMUTII

The beloved secret Vermouth cocktail recipe of Laava.

75ml (2½ oz)	Dry Vermouth, Noilly-Prat
22.5ml (¾ oz)	Amaro Montenegro
2 teaspoons	Butterscotch Liqueur, Bols
7.5ml (¼ oz)	Nardini alla Mandorla Almond Grappa
7.5ml (¼ oz)	Lemon Juice
1 teaspoon	*Subtle Sweetness Liqueur
Garnish: Lemon Wedge	

Stir all ingredients together with ice. Dump into a chilled white wine glass with a straw. Put a lemon wedge on the rim.

KING OF THE WORLD

When a snifter of fine cognac just isn't enough to express your superiority over the lesser humans of the world. A grand digestif after feasting on Lobster and Pheasant. A favorite at Laava for a particular bishop's lunch at the saintly sum of 100 euros each.

75ml (2½ oz)	Cognac, Pierre Ferrand *1840 1st Cru*
15ml (½ oz)	*Duality Cordial
15ml (½ oz)	Grapefruit Juice, strained
2 teaspoons	Egg White, whipped to facilitate measuring
7.5ml (¼ oz)	Lemon Juice, strained
1 teaspoon	Suze Gentian Liqueur
1 teaspoon	D.O.M. Benedictine
1 teaspoon	Aperol

Also: Cigar, preferably Cuban (see directions below)

Combine all ingredients in a shaker with ice to have ready. Chill a large red wine glass. Place a short piece of a cigar (ideally Cuban) on a metal plate and ignite it with a blowtorch. Invert the glass over it to collect smoke for 15-20 seconds. Now shake the mixture vigorously. Double strain into the glass.

CUBAN DICTATOR

This uses with the same procedure as above, but with a simple combination of two parts of aged Cuban rum (*e.g.* Ron Mulata 15 Year) to one part of very fine cognac (*e.g.* Hennessy *XO*). As before, invert the goblet over a lit cigar for 15-20 seconds to infuse it with smoke and then pour in the mixture of rum and cognac at room temperature (no ice this time). Castro himself would rise from the grave to applaud this.

Y

DR. LIVINGSTONE (I PRESUME)

Served in Laava's *Adventure Lounge* section in a custom made Tiki mug (see below). Ableforth's Bathtub Gin may also be used.

35ml (1¼ oz)	Salted Caramel Vodka, Stolichnaya
30ml (1 oz)	Gin, Monkey 47
30ml (1 oz)	Mango Liqueur, DeKuyper
60ml (2 oz)	Grapefruit Juice, preferably White
7.5ml (¼ oz)	Valhalla Liqueur
1 teaspoon	151-proof Rum
1 dash	Maraschino Liqueur, Luxardo
Garnish: Sprig of Mint	

In a blender, combine all of the ingredients except the maraschino liqueur and the overproof rum. Add 80g (2.8 oz) of ice cubes. Blend. Dump into a Tiki mug containing more ice. Add the overproof rum, maraschino liqueur, mint and a straw.

ARTIST MIKE GILBERT

Laava's mug with the visage of the famed 19th Century African explorer, Dr. Livingstone (complete with monacle) was created and produced by the artistic genius of Mike Gilbert. His elaborate, humorous and often amazing garnishes for Tiki cocktails are a constant delight to enthusiasts on several social media sites that are devoted to Tiki culture. We were honored to have his skill and wit become a part of Laava.

TROPICAL SPLASH

The Aperol Spritz is a very popular drink for summer in Finland. Some customers wanted something a little stronger and more in keeping with the tropical theme of Laava. Much too tame to be Tiki.

30ml (1 oz)	Light Rum, Plantation 3-Star
15ml (½ oz)	Apricot Brandy, Bols
15ml (½ oz)	Passionfruit Liqueur, Marie Brizard
15ml (½ oz)	Aperol
30ml (1 oz)	Tonic Water, Fever Tree *Mediterranean*
Garnish: Orange Peel, Pineapple Wedge	

Shake all ingredients except the tonic water with ice and then strain into a Zombie glass with plenty of ice cubes. Spritz the orange peel over the top and then drop it in. Slide a small fresh pineapple wedge on the rim and add a straw.

PLANET OF THE APRICOTS

The Duality Cordial harmonizes with the apricot liqueur and brandy to produce a new world of futuristically evolved flavors.

60ml (2 oz)	Spanish Brandy, Torres 10
15ml (½ oz)	Apricot Liqueur, Merlet
15ml (½ oz)	*Duality Cordial
15ml (½ oz)	Lemon Juice, strained
1 dash	Orange Bitters, Angostura brand
Garnish: Dried Apricot in Brandy (page 202) and a Cherry	

Shake all ingredients gently with ice cubes. Strain into a chilled Coupe glass. Add the garnish on a skewer.

MOWING THE GRASS

This one was never on the official menu. It became popular with a group of young hipsters who swore it was absolute bliss to sip while smoking marijuana, so they would order half a dozen of these and scurry away to hide in one of the large bathrooms for a couple of hours. Laava had 14 bathrooms, some of which occasionally doubled as clandestine enclaves for various uncondoned activities.

45ml (1½ oz)	Mezcal, Montelobos Joven
45ml (1½ oz)	D.O.M. Benedictine
7.5ml (¼ oz)	Amaro di Angostura
7.5ml (¼ oz)	Crème de Menthe, Tempus Fugit
3 dashes	Orange Bitters, Angostura brand
40ml (1.4 oz)	Tonic Water, Fever Tree *Mediterranean*

Combine all ingredients except the tonic water. Shake with ice and then strain into a chilled rocks glass with a single large ice cube. Add on the tonic water, plus a straw.

🍸

SIDE-CHARISMA

This began life as an uptown cousin of the well known Sidecar cocktail, but there was a delicious traffic accident along the way.

60ml (2 oz)	Cognac, Hennessy *VSOP*
22.5ml (¾ oz)	Vecchio Amaro Del Capo
22.5ml (¾ oz)	*Charisma Cordial
22.5ml (¾ oz)	Lime Juice, strained
Garnish: Luxardo Cherry	

Stir all ingredients with ice cubes. Strain into a chilled Coupe glass. Add the cherry on a skewer.

CHRISTMAS ANYTIME

Very much like Egg Nog, only with more spice and more alcohol. For a more interesting version, substitute 30ml (1 oz) of Advocaat in place of the cream and egg yolk.

22.5ml (¾ oz)	Cognac, Hennessy *VSOP*
22.5ml (¾ oz)	Vana Tallinn
15ml (½ oz)	D.O.M. Benedictine
15ml (½ oz)	Vecchio Amaro Del Capo
15ml (½ oz)	Heavy Cream (see text above)
1 medium	Egg Yolk
1 dash	Orange Bitters, Angostura brand

Garnish: Grated Nutmeg

Add all of the other ingredients and shake <u>well</u> with ice. Double strain into a chilled Martini glass. Grate a little nutmeg over the top.

Y

CLOUDS OVER VALHALLA

I created this for a cruise ship line in Finland to replace their simplistic cream and chocolate liqueur dessert cocktail.

22.5ml (¾ oz)	Vodka
15ml (½ oz)	Valhalla Liqueur
15ml (½ oz)	Dark Crème de Cacao, Tempus Fugit
1 teaspoon	Bigallet China China
1 dash	Aztek Chocolate Bitters, Fee Bros.
15g (½ oz)	Heavy Cream, semi-whipped

Combine all ingredients except the cream. Shake gently with cracked ice. Strain into an ice cold Cairn glass. Float the cream "cloud" using an open ruffle piping tip.

LAAVA SCORPION BOWL

This is the Laava version of the classic that I described in a full chapter in my previous book. This recipe includes Riesling wine in the way that Trader Vic made his Scorpion Bowl Punch back in the 1940's. This recipe is intended for two people to share.

45ml (1½ oz)	Gin, Tanqueray No. Ten
35ml (1¼ oz)	Aged Agricole Rhum, J. Bally was used
30ml (1 oz)	Cognac, Hennessy *VSOP*
15ml (½ oz)	Riesling Wine, Trimbach or Wolfberger
15ml (½ oz)	Sour Grapefruit Liqueur, DeKuyper
15ml (½ oz)	Curaçao, Merlet *Trois Citrus*
35ml (1¼ oz)	Lemon Juice (see note below)
2 teaspoons	Amaretto Syrup, 1883 brand
2 teaspoons	Pineapple Juice
1 teaspoon	Grenadine (the commercial product this time)
1 teaspoon	151-proof Rum

Garnishes: Gardenia Flower, Half Lime Shell

Combine all ingredients except the 151-proof rum with ice cubes. Shake and then dump entire the contents into a ceramic Scorpion Bowl. Place the half lime shell in the center well at the top. Add the 151 rum into the lime shell and ignite.

Note that the amount of lemon juice has been reduced to be in keeping with modern tastes. Long ago it was 60ml (2 oz) of lemon juice for the "sting" of the namesake scorpion. Then it was 45ml (1½ oz). Now this.

PALE RAINBOW

As with the Scorpion (previous page), Riesling wine harmonizes with gin. This is an unusual case where Chartreuse doesn't overwhelm the other ingredients. Each sip is a different experience.

35ml (1¼ oz)	Gin, Tanqueray No. Ten
22.5ml (¾ oz)	Riesling Wine, Trimbach or Wolfberger
22.5ml (¾ oz)	Yellow Chartreuse Liqueur
2 teaspoons	Maraschino Liqueur, ideally Maraska
7.5ml (¼ oz)	*Sicilian Bitter Lemon Cordial
1 teaspoon	Peach Liqueur, Giffard *Péche de Vigne*
1 teaspoon	Lemon Juice, strained
2-3 dashes	Bergamot Bitters

Combine all ingredients and stir with ice cubes. Strain into a chilled Martini glass straight up, or serve over ice if you prefer.

♼

YACHTSMAN

The slightly astringent cherry kirsch and white port are a natural pairing. This is relatively low in alcohol by international standards, but still quite strong compared to traditional Finnish cocktails.

60ml (2 oz)	Aged White Port, ideally Dalva
22.5ml (¾ oz)	Everclear, 120-proof
22.5ml (¾ oz)	*Pear Fassionola
15ml (½ oz)	Kirschwasser, Schwarzwälder
15ml (½ oz)	Lime Juice
4 dashes	Orange Bitters, Angostura brand

Combine all ingredients and stir with ice cubes. Strain over a large ice cube in a chilled Old Fashioned glass.

FIJI MERMAID

Served in a custom made ceramic mug. This is one twisted little curiousity, just as every Fiji Mermaid is.

30ml (1 oz)	Fiji Rum, Transcontinental was used
22.5ml (¾ oz)	Strega Liqueur
15ml (½ oz)	Pineapple Juice
15ml (½ oz)	Lemon Juice
2 teaspoons	*Duality Cordial
2 teaspoons	Heavy Cream
2-3 dashes	Orange Bitters, Angostura brand

Combine all ingredients and shake vigorously with ice cubes. Strain into a small chilled Tiki mug. Add a straw.

🍸

LAAVA'S HURRICANE

A dark version of the classic. While Licor 43 is not usually seen, it has always been an integral part of a Hurricane recipe in my book.

45ml (1½ oz)	Dark Rum, Gosling Black Seal
30ml (1 oz)	Overproof Rum, Hamilton 151
22.5ml (¾ oz)	*Fassionola
15ml (½ oz)	Licor 43
30ml (1 oz)	Lemon Juice
1-2 dashes	Allspice Dram
Garnish: Citrus Fruit Wedges, Luxardo Cherry, Paper Umbrella	

Combine all ingredients and shake with ice cubes. Strain over a lot of crushed ice in a Hurricane glass. Thread orange, lemon and lime wedges on a skewer with a cherry. Turn the paper umbrella inside out to simulate high wind. Add a straw.

RADAMA

Radama was a king of Madagascar, which is a large island of the eastern coast of Africa, famous for vanilla. The island was a French colony for centuries. The ingredients here are from Madagascar and France. The taste is complex, indescribable and lingering.

22.5ml (¾ oz)	Madagascar Rhum, Dzama *Cuvée Noire*
22.5ml (¾ oz)	Madagascar Vanilla Liqueur, Giffard
22.5ml (¾ oz)	Armagnac, *VSOP*
15ml (½ oz)	Lime Juice, strained
2 dashes	Grapefruit Bitters, Scrappy's

Combine all ingredients and stir with ice gently (do not over chill it). Strain into a crystal sherry glass.

Y

THE ROUGH END OF THE PINEAPPLE

An original Tiki style cocktail that makes use of two pineapple based liquors that naturally pair well with each other. One of the most popular cocktails at Laava and on the menu from the first day.

30ml (1 oz)	Pineapple Rum, Plantation *Stiggin's Fancy*
30ml (1 oz)	Spit-Roasted Pineapple Gin, That Boutique-y
15ml (½ oz)	Pineapple Juice
2 teaspoons	Banana Liqueur, Tempus Fugit (previously Bols)
7.5ml (¼ oz)	Dark Cuban Rum, Ron Mulata 15 Year
22.5ml (¾ oz)	Lemon Juice
1 teaspoon	*Falernum
Garnish: Fresh Pineapple Wedge	

Combine ingredients and shake with ice. Pour contents into a chilled rocks glass. Put the fruit on the rim and add a straw.

MOD SQUAD

This started out as copying a vibrant pink cocktail from a television show in 1969 that surprisingly—astoundingly—mentioned Fassionola. Here is an example of how Fassionola pairs well with Amaro Montenegro, as mentioned in the recipe in the appendix.

50ml (1¾ oz)	Vodka
30ml (1 oz)	Sour Rhubarb Liqueur, DeKuyper
15ml (½ oz)	Amaro Montenegro (see text above)
15ml (½ oz)	*Fassionola
7.5ml (¼ oz)	Lime Juice
½ teaspoon	Ginger Liqueur, Bols

Combine all ingredients and shake with cracked ice. Strain into a Martini glass. Play psychedelic music.

Y

PRETENDER TO THE THRONE

The key ingredient here is (obviously) this particular Sicilian dessert wine, which has strong notes of apricots and honey. It is a bit like a sweet Negroni, and was a huge hit among Italian Nonnas.

60ml (2 oz)	Colosi Malvasia Dell Lipari (see text above)
30ml (1 oz)	Gin, Tanqueray
15ml (½ oz)	Amaro Averna
1 teaspoon	Fernet Branca
2 dashes	Seville Orange Bitters, Scrappy's
Garnish: Orange Zest Curl	

Combine all ingredients. Stir with ice cubes. Strain into a chilled rocks glass with a single large ice cube. Then tightly coil the orange zest strip around a dowel or something and lay it on.

LAAVA BLACK MAGIC

A relative of the renowned Mai Kai cocktail from the 1950's. The odd measurements here are not a problem if you are using a scale, as we did at Laava (see page 1). This has been tested exhaustively, as shown by the counter on the Perfect Drink app, registering it has been made more than 1,800 times. The critically important lychee soda is available in many Asian grocery stores.

30ml (1 oz)	Columbian Rum, Dictador *VSOP* or *XO*
15ml (½ oz)	Dark Jamaican Rum, Smith & Cross
40ml (1.4 oz)	Espresso, Nescafé *Ristretto* (cooled first)
25ml (0.9 oz)	Pineapple Juice
17.5ml (0.6 oz)	Merlet Trois Citrus Curaçao
15ml (½ oz)	Lychee Soda, Rubicon brand
7.5ml (¼ oz)	Banana Liqueur, Bols
7.5ml (¼ oz)	Amaretto DiSaronno
1 teaspoon	Unicum Zwack
2 dashes	Angostura Bitters
Garnish: Orange Wheel	

Combine all ingredients and stir with ice. Strain into a red wine glass. Put the orange wheel on the rim and add a straw.

SOMETHING SIMPLE

Simple? Remember there are only *three* ingredients in a Negroni.

60ml (2 oz)	Cognac or Armagnac
15ml (½ oz)	Grand Marnier
2 teaspoons	Heering Cherry Liqueur
1 dash	Angostura Bitters

Add all to a rocks glass with a single large ice cube. Stir.

PASSION ISLAND

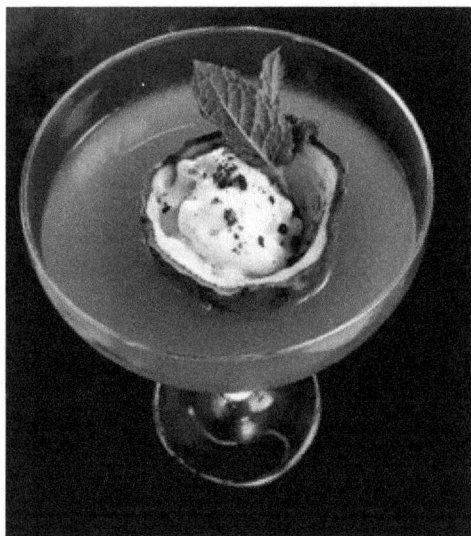

This consists of a rum cocktail with an "island" floating on it that's filled with a liqueur-cream mixture, as shown in the photo here.

The recipe for the cream filling (shown below) makes enough for six of these cocktails and uses three passion fruit, which works out perfectly because you need half an empty shell for each drink. Best to make the filling a day ahead.

3 whole	Passion Fruit, about 30g (1 oz) each
225ml (8 oz)	Heavy Cream
60g (2 oz)	Coconut Nectar, blonde
45ml (1½ oz)	D.O.M. Benedictine
2 ½ Tablespoons	Lechithin, ground into powder
3 sheets	Gelatin
3 Medium	Egg Whites

Cut the passion fruit in halves and scrape out the contents of each into a sauce pan. Refrigerate the shells for later use. Add all of the other ingredients except the gelatine and egg whites to the sauce pan. Begin heating gently. Meanwhile soften the gelatin sheets in cold water. When the temperature in the pan is 80°C (176°F), whisk in the gelatin. When it is dissolved, take it off the heat and pour into a pressure canister. Let it cool for 30 minutes or more, then add the egg whites. Close it up and charge with one nitrous cylinder. Shake vigorously. Refrigerate for a minimum of least 3 hours before use. Makes 6 cocktails.

For each individual Passion Island cocktail...

45ml (1½ oz)	Passoã Passion Fruit Liqueur
30ml (1 oz)	D.O.M. Benedictine
15ml (½ oz)	Aged Martinique Rhum, J. Bally was used
2 teaspoons	Lime Juice, strained

Garnish: Reserved Passion Fruit Shell, Liqueur Cream (previous recipe on opposite page), Large Flake Black Salt, Mint Sprig

Combine all ingredients. Shake with ice and then double strain into a chilled Coupe glass. Fill one of the passion fruit shells with the aerosol liquer-cream, then add a mint leaf to it and sprinkle with a little black salt. Serve with a dessert spoon.

Y

UNIVERSAL ANTIDOTE

This was used for customers who asked for something new "just for them" and named one or two ingredients they liked. The result is usually quite good. For vodka or gin, use orange or grapefruit bitters. For rum or cognac use Angostura. For bourbon use Boker's. The "Other Named Ingredient" could be anything from Jägermeister to Crème de Menthe. If they can't name anything else, use either Grand Marnier or Heering. Many customers who make special requests at the bar are unaware that there may be dozens of other orders streaming in from the dining rooms and that time is limited.

45ml (1½ oz)	Vodka, Gin, Rum, Cognac or Bourbon
15ml (½ oz)	Other Named Ingredient (see text above)
15ml (½ oz)	*Unicorn Matrix Zero
15ml (½ oz)	Grapefruit Juice
1 dash	Bitters (see text above)

Combine all ingredients. Shake with ice and serve straight up or on the rocks, as desired.

SPIRAL / I DID IT AGAIN

This was originally named a Spiral, but the bartenders hated this drink more than life itself, owing to the list of 12 ingredients that makes it take so long to prepare. One night when an order came in from one of the dining rooms for 22 of these, one bartender quit on the spot, shouting some rather obscene language about it being impossible to make so many of these and serve them all at the same time with all of these finicky ingredients. It really wasn't, though. We just lined up 11 shakers and put the ingredients for two drinks in each one and did it again and again and again. So the drink was renamed. Most bartenders are used to simple three or four ingredient drinks, and are also not used to dozens of orders arriving at the same time. The flavor is a an incredibly complex cascade of sweetness, sourness, mysterious fruits, hints of exotic spices and just a touch of bitterness with a very long finish.

45ml (1½ oz)	Gin, Tanqueray
22.5ml (¾ oz)	Grapefruit Juice, strained
15ml (½ oz)	Aperol
15ml (½ oz)	Grand Marnier
2 teaspoons	Crème de Banana, Tempus Fugit (Bols originally)
7.5ml (¼ oz)	Lemon Juice, strained
1 teaspoon	Overproof White Rum, Wray & Nephew
½ teaspoon	Crème de Cassis
½ teaspoon	Crème de Noyeaux
½ teaspoon	Bigallet China China
½ teaspoon	Apricot Liqueur, Merlet
2 dashes	Grapefruit Bitters, Scrappy's

Garnish: Lime Peel

Combine all ingredients. Stir and strain into a chilled Coupe glass. Use a zester to cut a long, thin strip of the lime peel over the top of the drink, then curl it up and drop it in.

Y

Cordials and Liqueurs

The terms cordial and liqueur are often used interchangeably, but technically a cordial may or may not contain alcohol, while a liqueur always does. Also, liqueurs are always sweetened and cordials are not always sweetened. This is an inclusive guide to all of the original cordials and liqueurs called for in this book.

In many recipes here, 120-proof Everclear is called for with a note that you may substitute vodka. You *can*, but the results will not be as good. Try to use Everclear if at all possible.

BARLEY BASE

This was part of the original Orgeat Syrup from centuries ago. It is used as an ingredient in several of the recipes ahead.

30g (1 oz)	Barley Flour

1. Put the barley flour in a pot with 200ml (7 oz) water. Whisk.

2. Bring to a simmer with frequent stirring. Within 5 minutes the mixture will be very thick. It is absolutely vital that you stir this frequently or it will burn at the bottom.

3. Cool to room temperature. Then bottle and refrigerate. This is your barley base and enough for several batches of orgeat and other recipes.

ULTRA RICH CRÈME DE CACAO

This was inspired by Mozart Black (see page 45), and it is similar but not quite as sweet, but extremely rich in chocolate flavor. You can use this to replace Mozart Black in any recipe with excellent results. It is much darker than Tempus Fugit's Cacao.

65g (2.3 oz)	Muscovado sugar
65g (2.3 oz)	Sugar, white granulated
65g (2.3 oz)	Cacao (100% pure cocoa powder)
100ml (3.5 oz)	Water
300ml (10.5 oz)	Vodka
60g (2 oz)	Agave Syrup
15ml (½ oz)	Plantation OFTD rum (69% ABV)
2 teaspoons	Vanilla Extract

1. Heat the two sugars in a pan on a low setting gently with occasional stirring to keep it from burning. It will be difficult to stir at first, and sugar will stick to the spatula, but just keep at it until the temperature reaches 143°C (290°F). An infrared thermometer is ideal for monitoring this.

2. Now remove it from the heat temporarily and add the cacao. Stir this in as best you can for about a minute, cooking the cacao in the hot caramel briefly.

3. Add the water and return it to the heat. Bring to a simmer. Stir until it is nearly all dissolved, which will be 3-4 minutes.Turn off the heat and let it cool for about 2 minutes, stirring occasionally.

4. Use a stick blender to help dissolve chunks of caramel. Then pass it through a fine mesh sieve. Discard any solids.

5. Add the vodka, agave syrup, Plantation OFTD rum and the vanilla extract. Now pass it through a Chinois. Mix and bottle. Refrigerate if keeping for more than about 2 weeks.

MONTEREY LIQUEUR

This peculiar liqueur pairs especially well with tequilas of all types (blanco through anejo). Tequila is intrinsically Mexican, and the two essential flavors of most Mexican cuisine are chilies and cumin. So it is not surprising to find that this liqueur is a natural to pair with chili-infused vodkas, mezcal, and especially Ancho Reyes' Poblano (green) and original *Ancho (brown) liqueurs. However cumin is not the only flavor going on here, so this will also add an unusual complexity to dark rum drinks when used judiciously.

250ml (8.8 oz)	Apple Juice
60g (2 oz)	Muscovado Sugar
1 Tablespoon	Cumin Seeds, whole
1 pod	Star Anise, broken into pieces
1 teaspoon	Orange Zest, grated
45ml (1½ oz)	Madeira Wine
45ml (1½ oz)	Barbados Rum, Plantation
1 teaspoon	Gammel Dansk (optional)
¼ teaspoon	Angostura Bitters

1. Combine the apple juice, muscovado sugar, cumin seeds, star anise and orange zest in a sauce pan.

2. Heat on medium-low to bring to a simmer. Maintain at a simmer for about 20 minutes.

3. Cool at room temperature 5 minutes.

4. Pass through a fine mesh sieve tamis. Discard solids.

5. Add the Madeira, Barbados rum, Gammel Dansk (recommended but not absolutely essential) and Angostura bitters. Use a funnel to transfer to a clean bottle. Best kept refrigerated, but not essential.

* Incidentally, ancho is the name given to dried poblano chilies, which are otherwise green when fresh.

GOLDEN LIME CORDIAL

This can replace Rose's Lime Cordial in most cocktails with superior results in many cases, although there are more bitter notes here, so it will depend some. For example an improved classic **Gimlet** *can be made with a mix of this liqueur, lime juice and gin in the ratio of 1:1:3. The unusual complexity of this cordial also works magic on many cocktails in teaspoon and even half-teaspoon amounts. This is especially true of tequila cocktails, but certainly not limited to those.*

50g (1.75 oz)	Lime Shell, ground (see text)
75ml (2.65 oz)	Orange Juice
75g (2.65 oz)	Sugar
50ml (1.75 oz)	Apple Juice
½ teaspoon	Basil, dried
25ml (0.9 oz)	Everclear, 120 proof (or substitute vodka)

1. Use limes that have already been juiced (the shells). Cut up into small chunks with a knife.

2. Grind the pieces in a food processor. Do not use a high powered blender such as a Vitamix. The rind will not chop up very much, but that's fine. You have liberated the natural oils.

3. Scrape out 50g (1.75 oz) of the ground up pulp into a sauce pan. Add all of the other ingredients except the Everclear (or vodka).

4. Bring to an actual boil, then immediately reduce the heat. Keep it at a slow simmer for 5 minutes.

5. Cool at room temperature for another 5 minutes.

6. Pass through a very fine mesh tamis.

7. Add the Everclear (or vodka). Stir and bottle. Refrigeration will maintain freshness longer, but it is not necessary.

OLD FASHIONED ORGEAT

This was originally a porridge for the sick and elderly and had nothing to do with cocktails. The original recipe goes back to the 18th century. This is quite close to the original, but prepared using milled barley which speeds the process up by hours. Because this will be too thick to pour, it is best transferred by a spoon. This is different from commercial orgeat syrups, most of which are closer to the Creme de Noyaux recipe on the next page, but without the food coloring. **The Mai Tai recipe in this book was developed before I began using this syrup. Don't substitute this. Use Giffard's Orgeat for the Mai Tai to obtain the correct balance.**

50g (1.75 oz)	Barley Base (page 171)
90g (3 oz)	Almonds, ground
100g (3.5 oz)	Sugar, white granulated
½ teaspoon	Almond Extract

1. Put the ground almonds and sugar in a pot. Add 250ml (8.8 oz) water and the Barley Base.

2. Bring to a simmer. Continue heating for 5 minutes, stirring often.

3. Let cool for 5 minutes at room temperature.

4. Stir in the almond extract.

4. Rub through an ordinary wire mesh sieve. Discard the solids that did not pass.

5. Now rub through a Chinois or the finest screen of a tamis. The reason you passed it through the first time was to keep the finer screen from becoming clogged.

6. Refrigerate this for 24 hours before use. Keep refrigerated. Due to the barley, it will spoil at room temperature.

✦

CREME DE NOYAUX

This is classic liqueur popular in the 1950's and 1960's, but seldom seen these days until Tempus Fugit reintroduced it. The flavor is intense almonds and very sweet. It is also bright red, which is usually an important aspect for cocktails calling for this. The most famous cocktail being the Pink Squirrel. This recipe is very similar to the Tempus Fugit product in taste, but thicker because it is not distilled. The viscosity is unlikely to be an issue in any cocktail.

150g (5.3 oz)	Almonds, ground
300g (10.6 oz)	Sugar
40ml (1.4 oz)	DiSaronno Amaretto liqueur
10 drops	Almond Extract
10 drops	Orange Blossom Water
¼ teaspoon	Red Food Coloring, powdered

1. Put 300ml (10.6 oz) water into a small pot or sauce pan. Add the ground almonds and sugar.

2. Bring to a simmer with occasional stirring. Maintain at a simmer for about 10 minutes.

3. Let the mixture steep at room temperature for another 10 minutes.

4. Rub through a fine mesh sieve tamis. Discard the solids.

5. Now pass again through a Chinois. The reason you passed it through the tamis first was to keep the Chinois from being clogged.

6. Add the Amaretto, almond extract and orange blossom water. Mix.

7. Transfer to a bottle using a funnel. Add the red food color. Stopper the bottle and agitate it to mix until the color has fully developed.

8. Refrigeration is not necessary, but cold will help retain flavor.

FALERNUM

This is an important ingredient in many Tiki recipes. There are many commercial products called Falernum. Some are non-alcoholic syrups such as Monin's product. Some can have alcohol but be very light in flavor and have no texture at all, such as John D. Taylor's Velvet Falernum (11% alcohol). Still others are so strong that they damage the balance of the cocktail. This recipe will produce a flavorful cordial with some milky texture. The Becherovka addition will boost the herbal notes.

180g (6.3 oz)	Sugar
60g (2 oz)	Almonds, ground
60ml (2 oz)	Lime Juice, fresh
30g (1 oz)	Ginger, fresh, cut in thin slices with the peel
30g (1 oz)	Barley Base (page 171)
1 Tablespoon	Lime Zest, grated fine
1 teaspoon	Allspice, whole
1 teaspoon	Cloves, whole
100ml (3.5 oz)	Light Rum, Plantation 3-star
2 teaspoons	Becherovka (optional)

1. You do not need to peel the ginger, but slice it very thin.

2. In a small pot, combine all of the ingredients except the rum and Becherovka (if you are using it). Also add 300ml (10.6 oz) water.

3. Bring to a simmer while stirring. Maintain at a simmer 10 minutes.

4. Remove from the heat and let steep for 5-6 minutes.

5. Pass through a sieve. Discard the solids.

6. Add the rum and Becherovka (if using it) and stir.

7. Rub through a fine mesh sieve resting on a funnel leading into a bottle, then once again, discard the solids.

7. Bottle and refrigerate. It will spoil at room temperature.

+

SPICED DATE LIQUEUR

This is a potent flavor enhancer when used in small amounts. Because dates and cardamom are two of the subtle background notes in aged dark rums, this lets you amp up those notes and take control of your rum's profile. Also, combine this with vodka in the ratio of 1:7 and you have a Spiced Date Vodka that is useful in many cocktails.

140g (5 oz)	Dates, fresh
60g (2 oz)	Muscovado Sugar
1 pod	Star Anise, broken up into pieces
3/4 teaspoon	Cardamom, ground
60ml (2 oz)	Barbados Rum, Plantation or better

1. For best results, use fresh dates and not dried ones. Slice each one open and remove the pit.

2. Grind the pitted dates in a food processor.

3. Scrape out the pulp into a sauce pan. Add 170ml (6 oz) of water, the muscovado sugar, the star anise and the ground cardamom.

4. Bring to a simmer. Keep it at a slow simmer for 2 minutes. Stir!

5. Cool at room temperature for another 3 minutes. Don't let it cool too much or it will not pass cleanly through the sieve in the next step.

6. Rub through a large regular wire sieve over a bowl. Discard the solids that wouldn't pass. Be sure to scrape the botton of the sieve.

7. Transfer to a blender or the cup of a stick blender. Add the rum and blend to purée for about a minute.

8. Pass through a Chinois. Transfer to a bottle using a funnel. Keep refrigerated to retain freshness and prevent spoilage.

RED ELK CORDIAL

This may be served mixed with gin as an aperitif, especially before a meal of roasted elk or other venison. It segues beautifully with a deep red wine served next or alongside the entrée. Alternatively as a digestive served neat like port wine in a small stemmed glass, kept chilled in the refrigerator. As an ingredient in a cocktail, this has astringency from the tannin in the wine, so it must be used in moderation. The citrus, juniper and coriander notes make it a natural pairing for gin cocktails. It is also a great support player for almost any cocktail containing maraschino liqueur.

150ml (5.3 oz)	Pomegranate-Apple Juice mix (100% juice)
50ml (1.75 oz)	Red Wine, dry (cabernet and/or pinot noir)
50g (1.75 oz)	Sugar
2 teaspoons	Lemon Zest, grated fine
½ teaspoon	Coriander Seeds, whole
3 whole	Java Long Pepper or ½ t Black Peppercorns
½ teaspoon	Juniper Berries, whole
30ml (1 oz)	Everclear, 120 proof (or substitute vodka)
½ teaspoon	Campari

1. Be sure to use juice with no added sugar. In a small pot combine all of the ingredients except the Everclear (or vodka) and Campari.

2. Bring to a simmer while stirring occassionally. Maintain at a simmer for 5 minutes.

3. Remove from the heat and let steep for another 5 minutes.

4. Pass through a very fine mesh tamis.

5. Add the Everclear (or vodka) and the Campari.

9. Transfer to a bottle. Refrigerate if you are going to keep this for more than a few days.

✦

DARK BANANA LIQUEUR

This is a copy of Tempus Fugit's product. This is far superior to most commercial banana liqueurs such as Bols, DeKuyper, etc. Tempus Fugit's product is still slightly better because they have precision temperature control and other equipment no one has at home, but their product is quite expensive and this will work perfectly in any recipe as long as you made it carefully. Know ahead of time that this is not an easy recipe to make. Even though I have made it many times and have decades of professional experience, I still fail about 20% of the time, generally due to slightly burning it. The margin of error is razor thin when you do not have a computer controlled precision Thermomix that can operate under high vacuum. Still, bananas and sugar are not expensive ingredients, and you will know if you succeeded of failed before you commit to investing the other more expensive ingredients here, so practice makes perfect, as they say.

180g (6.5 oz)	Banana, very, very ripe
60g (2 oz)	Muscovado Sugar
100g (3.5 oz)	Sugar
30ml (1 oz)	Everclear, 120 proof (or substitute vodka)
15ml (½ oz)	Plantation OFTD rum (69% ABV)
¼ teaspoon	Vanilla extract

1. Peel and cut the bananas into large pieces.

2. In a small pot place the two sugars and the bananas. Heat on a low setting with occasional light stirring until a temperature of 93°C (198°F) has been reached. Use a low heat. I can't stress that enough. This may seem picky to you, but that's how making a caramel works. You have to hit the exact temperature. When it gets close, lower the heat even more. Break up the bananas a little (don't mash them) and

push them into the caramel as it forms and tends to push the bananas up and out of the caramel. This will take at least 20 minutes of attention if you are going slow enough. The success of this recipe depends entirely on this stage. Too much and it will be burnt and nasty. Not enough and it won't taste like the Tempus Fugit product. If it actually smells burnt, start over because you rushed it with too much heat. You need to know the difference between deep caramelization and burnt sugar. The former is a fantastic product; the latter is a very sticky mess that you will be scraping out into the trash.

3. Now add 100ml (3.5 oz) water. Bring to a simmer. Maintain at that simmer for 10 minutes with frequent stirring.

4. Remove from the heat and let stand at room temperature for 3 to 4 minutes.

5. Pass through a fine mesh tamis. Get as much liquid through as you can, but do not crush the banana pieces or your liqueur will be cloudy. Discard the solids, or save them to bake into banana muffins or banana bread. At any rate, the solids are of no further use in this recipe.

6. Add the Everclear (or vodka), the rum and the vanilla extract.

7. Stir and bottle. Refrigeration will maintain freshness longer, but it is not necessary.

ANGRY MONKEY SAYS

Expect that this will not go perfectly the first couple of times. This is a deceptively difficult recipe due to the exact temperature and times required for optimum results. Still, it can be done and it is well worth the effort!

DUALITY CORDIAL

This is especially well matched to Cachaça and Pisco cocktails. Try it in a Caipirinha in place of some of the citrus and sugar for a more complex cocktail. For those who enjoy some funk, try the **Laava Haitian Divorce**. *Mix equal parts of Duality Cordial with pineapple juice, lime juice, gin and Clairin (or much better, the Ghana rum shown on page 91). Add a little Angostura, too.*

100ml (3.5 oz)	Blood Orange Juice
30ml (1 oz)	Pineapple Juice
22.5g (¾ oz)	Honey (Licorice Honey ideally)
1 teaspoon	Lemon Zest
3cm (1 inch)	Cinnamon Stick, broken into pieces
½ teaspoon	White Peppercorns, whole
½ teaspoon	Fennel Seeds, whole
140g (5 oz)	Sugar
60ml (2 oz)	Vodka
5 drops	Lime Oil

1. Combine all of the ingredients except the vodka and lime oil in a sauce pan.

2. Gently heat to a simmer on a medium-low setting. Stir occasionally and maintain at a simmer for 3-4 minutes.

4. Remove from heat. After 5 minutes add the vodka and stir.

3. Let stand for 5 more minutes (still at room temperature).

5. Strain through the finest mesh of a tamis or use a Chinois. Discard the solids that did not pass through.

6. Transfer to a stoppered bottle using a funnel.

7. Add the lime oil and swirl to mix. Keep refrigerated to retain freshness and prevent spoilage.

✦

SUBTLE SWEETNESS LIQUEUR

Two applications for this are simulating Old Tom gins and to enhance gin notes in a drink. This can also tame the harshness of some amari. When a recipe calls for simple syrup, this is something to consider as a substitute for improving complexity.

60ml (2 oz)	Orange Juice
30ml (1 oz)	Cranberry Juice, Ocean Spray
22.5ml (¾ oz)	Grapefruit Juice
1 Tablespoon	Grapefruit zest, grated
2 teaspoons	Lime Juice
6 whole	Juniper Berries, crushed
6 whole	Allspice Berries, crushed
2 teaspoons	Muscovado Sugar
160g (5.6 oz)	Sugar
60ml (2 oz)	Everclear, 120 proof (or substitute vodka)
7.5ml (¼ oz)	Valhalla Liqueur (see text above)
3 drops	Lemon Oil
1 drop	Orange Oil

1. Combine all of the ingredients except the Everclear, Valhalla, lemon oil and orange oil in a small pot.

2. Heat gently to bring to a simmer with occasional stirring. Maintain at a simmer for about 4 minutes.

3. Remove from the heat and let steep at room temperature for 5 minutes or so.

4. Strain through the finest mesh of a tamis. Discard solids that do not pass through.

5. Add the Everclear (or vodka) and Valhalla (if you have it).

6. Transfer to a stopped bottle using a funnel.

7. Add the lemon oil and orange oil and swirl to mix. Refrigerate if you are going to keep this for a long time to preserve the flavor.

BRAMBLE LIQUEUR

Like the Subtle Sweetness on the previous page, this also smooths the harshness of amari and anise liqeuers. For the full effect with amari, an equal portion of Bramble is a good starting point to experiment with. This is also an excellent partner with Crème de Cassis and berry liqueurs such as Chambord.

120ml (4.2 oz)	Cranberry Juice, Ocean Spray
30ml (1 oz)	Pineapple Juice
15g (½ oz)	Grapefruit Juice
140g (5 oz)	Sugar
1 teaspoon	Lime Zest, grated fine
60ml (2 oz)	Light Rum, Plantation 3-Star
15ml (½ oz)	Everclear, 120 proof (or substitute vodka)
1 drop	Orange Oil

1. In a pot or saucepan, combine all ingredients except for the rum, the Everclear (or vodka) and the orange oil.

2. Bring to a slow boil on a medium-low heat (more than a simmer, but not a rolling boil.

3. Cook for 15 minutes with occasional stirring.

4. This mixture will become thick and gooey when it cools, so while it is still hot, pass it through the finest mesh of a tamis and then immediately into a bottle using a funnel.

5. Add the rum, the Everclear (or vodka) and the orange oil to the bottle. You will likely need to shake it to dissolve the contents completely.

6. This does not need refrigeration. Keep out of direct sunlight.

EARTH TONES CORDIAL

Even though pears are a major component of this, the resulting flavor has only subtle pear notes. It can take the place of brown or demerara sugar syrup in many cocktails to add complexity.

250g (8.8 oz)	Pear Halves, canned
90g (3 oz)	Sugar
60g (2 oz)	Muscovado Sugar
1 teaspoon	Cloves, whole
1/2 teaspoon	Lavender, dried (culinary grade)
30ml (1 oz)	Everclear 120 proof (or substitute vodka)
1 drop	Orange Oil

1. Drain a can of pear halves on a sieve. Discard the packing liquid.

2. Put the muscovado and the sugar in a large pot or saucepan. Place the pear halves on top, cut-side down. Sprinkle the cloves over this.

3. Set on a low heat. The sugars will begin to bubble. Stir this a little, not disturbing the pears. Adjust the heat if needed to prevent any burning. The sugar must caramelize slowly.

4. After 10 minutes, turn the pear halves over and cut each piece in half lengthwise with the edge of a spatula. Continue heating and stirring.

5. After another 5 minutes, cut the pear pieces in half crosswise. Stir.

6. After 15 more minutes add 90ml (3 oz) water and the lavender. Increase heat to bring to a simmer. Stir occasionally for 5 minutes.

7. Cool for a couple of minutes, then pass through the finest screen of a tamis. Add the Everclear (or vodka). Stir.

8. Transfer to a bottle using a funnel. Add the orange oil. Keep refrigerated to retain freshness.

HERBAL WONDER LIQUEUR

The lavendar and dried rose have to be culinary grade. It may be difficult to acquire these ingredients in a store, so look online. It's an outstanding product that pairs especially well with dark rums.

15ml (½ oz)	Pineapple Juice
15ml (½ oz)	Vodka
15g (½ oz)	Molasses, ideally "Almost Rum" brand
1 teaspoon	Lime Zest
½ teaspoon	Fenugreek
½ teaspoon	Coriander Seeds
½ teaspoon	Green Peppercorns, whole
¼ teaspoon	Mint, dried
¼ teaspoon	Lovage, dried
¼ teaspoon	Fennel Pollen
¼ teaspoon	Lavender, dried
1	Dried Rose, crumbled
140g (5 oz)	Sugar
60ml (2 oz)	Everclear, 120 proof (or substitute vodka)
1 teaspoon	Cinnamon Liqueur, preferably Fireball
5 drops	Grapefruit Oil

1. Combine all of the ingredients except the Everclear, Fireball liqueur and grapefruit oil in a small pot. Add 60ml (2 oz) of water.

2. Heat gently to bring to a simmer with occasional stirring. Maintain at a simmer for about 4 minutes.

3. Remove from the heat and let steep at room temperature for 5 minutes or so.

4. Strain through the finest mesh of a tamis. Discard solids that do not pass through.

5. Add the Everclear and Fireball liqueur.

6. Transfer to a stoppered bottle using a funnel.

7. Add the grapefruit oil and swirl to combine. Store refrigerated to maintain freshness.

TULIP CUP CORDIAL

This is one of my favorite cordials for contributing subtle spice notes. It is important to use pure licorice powder, also known as lakrits. Genever is a Dutch type of gin that is coarse in taste, for lack of a better description. This cordial pairs well with all liquors.

120ml (4.2 oz)	Ruby Grapefruit Juice with bits of pulp (no seeds)
15ml (½ oz)	Genever
2 ½ teaspoons	Grapefruit zest, grated
1 teaspoon	Licorice Root, powdered
½ t	Nutmeg, ground
½ t	Allspice, ground
¼ t	Cloves, ground
170g (6 oz)	Sugar
30ml (1 oz)	Everclear, 120 proof (or substitute vodka)
2 drops	Lemon Oil

1. In a small pot combine all of the ingredients except the Everclear (or vodka) and the lemon oil.

2. Bring to a slow simmer. Maintain at a simmer for 4 minutes with occasional stirring, then take off the heat and rest for 4 minutes.

3. Pour through the finest mesh of a tamis, collecting the liquid in a bowl. In this case do not rub the tamis. Accept that there will be some waste. Discard the solids that collected on the tamis screen.

4. Stir in the Everclear (or vodka). Then transfer to a wide-mouth jar.

5. Add the lemon oil. Put the lid on and invert to mix. Let stand at room temperature for 24 hours.

6. Carefully pour off the clear liquid, leaving the sediment behind. This is why a wide mouth jar is better, so you can pour it off without disturbing the sediment. Now transfer the clear liquid to a bottle.

7. If you are going to keep this for a long time then refrigerate it to preserve the freshness.

CHARISMA CORDIAL

As in the case of the Tulip Cup cordial on the previous page, this plays well with many different base liquors. This is especially intriguing as a 1:1 mixture with Lillet Blanc.

60ml (2 oz)	Orange Juice
25ml (0.9 oz)	Lime Juice
25ml (0.9 oz)	Grapefruit Juice
30ml (1 oz)	Vermouth, Dry French
15ml (½ oz)	Crème de Cassis
1 teaspoon	Grapefruit Zest, grated
1 teaspoon	Lime Zest, grated
½ teaspoon	Mint, dried
140g (5 oz)	Sugar
45ml (1½ oz)	Everclear 120 proof (or substitute vodka)
8 drops	Orange Oil

1. Combine all ingredients in a small pot or saucepan, except the Everclear (or vodka) and the orange oil.

2. Bring to a slow simmer with frequent stirring. Maintain at a simmer for about 4 minutes.

3. Remove from the heat and let steep for 15 minutes at room temperature.

4. Pass through the finest mesh of a tamis. Discard the solids.

5. Add the Everclear (or vodka) and stir.

6. Transfer to a bottle using a funnel. Add the orange oil and swirl to combine. It doesn't need refrigeration, but if you are going to keep it for a long time then cold will keep it tasting fresh for longer.

SICILIAN BITTER LEMON CORDIAL

This is a good addition to Limoncello in many cocktails. It is also especially well suited to pairing with Averna Amaro.

60ml (2 oz)	Lemon Juice
30ml (1 oz)	Orange Juice
2 teaspoons	Lemon Zest
1½ teaspoons	Fennel Seeds
1 teaspoon	Marjoram, dried
140g (5 oz)	Sugar
60ml (2 oz)	Vodka
½ teaspoon	Fernet Branca
4 drops	Lemon Oil

1. In a small pot or saucepan, combine all of the ingredients except the vodka, the Fernet Branca and the lemon oil.

2. Heat gently with stirring for about 5 minutes to dissolve all of the sugar well. Do not boil.

3. Cool at room temperature for 3-4 minutes,

4. Add the vodka and stir.

5. Pass through the finest mesh of a tamis. Discard the solids.

6. Transfer to a bottle with a funnel. Then add the Fernet Branca and the lemon oil. Swirl to combine.

7. Stopper and store refrigerated.

BITTER CHERRY CORDIAL

Inspired by Cynar, but not as bitter. Especially well suited to bourbon, rye and cognac. The flavor is subtle and layered.

100g (3.5 oz)	Artichoke Leaf Tips
160g (5.6 oz)	Lemon Shell, spent
160g (5.6 oz)	Orange Shell, spent
50ml (1.75 oz)	Orange Juice, fresh
50ml (1.75 oz)	Vodka
45g (1.5 oz)	Dark Corn Syrup
4cm (1.5 inch)	Cinnamon Stick, broken into pieces
2 whole	Star Anise pods, broken into pieces
30ml (1 oz)	Heering Cherry Liqueur

1. When cooking fresh artichokes, you should always clip the tops of the leaves before cooking. This will require the leaf tips from between two and four artichokes, depending on their size.

2. Coarsely chop the previously squeezed lemon and orange shells. Add these to a pressure cooker along with the artichoke leaf tips.

3. Add 225ml (7.9 oz) water and all of the rest of the ingredients except for the Heering.

4. Bring to a simmer, then seal the pressure cooker. Maintain just barely at pressure for 20 minutes.

5. Cool at room temperature for 5 minutes, then open the cooker.

6. Pass the contents through a coarse sieve and then through the finest mesh of a tamis.

7. Transfer to a nonstick skillet. Bring to a slow simmer. Do not boil vigorously. Maintain a slow simmer for 15 minutes.

8. Pass through the finest mesh of a tamis again. The weight should now be about 100g (3.5 oz). Now add the Heering.

9. Transfer to a bottle using a funnel. Keep refrigerated to retain freshness.

BITTER ORANGE CORDIAL

This was inspired by a seldom seen Italian liqueur called Borsi. After seeing how useful it is in cocktails, but unable to obtain another bottle, this substitute was created. It is not the same, because this is not distilled, but it works nicely in many cocktails.

120ml (4.2 oz)	Orange Juice, fresh
60ml (2 oz)	Vodka
60g (2 oz)	Orange Peel (see Step #1 below)
40g (1.4 oz)	Sugar
½ teaspoon	Seville Orange Bitters, Scrappy's
2 drops	Orange Oil

1. Use a vegetable peeler to remove the outside zest of the oranges, with only a little of the white pith left on each strip. Then run a knife through the peels to cut them up into small pieces roughly in the shape of squares.

2. Combine all of the ingredients in a food processor except the orange bitters and the orange oil.

3. Blend furiously to homogenize as best as possible.

4. Pass through a Chinois or the finest mesh of a tamis. Discard the solids.

5. Transfer to a bottle. Add the orange bitters and orange oil. Swirl to combine, then stopper. Refrigerate if you are going to keep this for a long time.

✦

VIC'S RUM NASTOYKA

This was not called a nastoyka, but that's what it is. **If you can't get hibiscus and vanilla tea, use plain hibiscus tea such as The Tao of Tea, and add a little vanilla bean pulp to it.**

75ml (2.6 oz)	Light Rum, Plantation 3-Star
30g (1 oz)	Raisins
½ teaspoon	Hibiscus & Vanilla Tea, Forsman (see above)
1 whole	Star Anise Pod, broken up

1. Combine in a jar and shake daily for at least a few days, and maintaining this for 2 weeks is even better.

2. Strain off solids and bottle. No refrigeration is needed.

✦

FASSIONOLA

As in the previous recipe, this also uses Hibiscus & Vanilla Tea by Forsman. Better than any commercial Fassionola that I know of.

100g (3½ oz)	Strawberry Preserves, St. Dalfour
70g (2½ oz)	Passionfruit Pulp
60ml (2 oz)	Pineapple Juice
45g (1½ oz)	Blueberries, fresh
90g (3 oz)	Sugar
1 teaspoon	Hibiscus & Vanilla Tea, Forsman
60ml (2 oz)	120 proof Everclear, or substitute vodka

1. Put all ingredients except the Everclear (or vodka) in a saucepan.

2. Add 90ml (3 oz) water. Bring to a simmer on a low heat until all of the sugar is dissolved. After about 5 minutes, use a stick blender on it.

3. Cook for 3-4 minutes more, then pass through a Chinois or very fine mesh sieve. Bottle. Add the Everclear or vodka. Refrigerate if you are going to keep it for over a week. Freeze portions for longer storage.

PEAR FASSIONOLA

This is related to Fassionola (see previous page) but not a substitute. The taste is different and sweeter.

150g (5.3 oz)	Pears, canned (drained well)
120g (4.2 oz)	Sugar
60ml (2 oz)	Orange Juice
30g (1 oz)	Passionfruit Pulp
30g (1 oz)	Blueberries, fresh
1 whole	Star Anise Pod, broken up
6 whole	Cloves (the spice)
45ml (1½ oz)	Vodka

1. Combine all ingredients except the vodka in a sauce pan. Bring to a simmer. Maintain at a simmer for 15 minutes.

2. Pass through the finest mesh of a tamis. Bottle and then add the vodka. Refrigerate if you are going to keep it for more than a week.

CLOUDY PEAR VODKA

*This is an substitute for **Absolut Pears Vodka** in terms of the flavor being acceptable in most cocktails, but it has some opalescence that may not be desirable, depending on the recipe.*

10 parts	Pears, fresh, peeled and sliced
10 parts by weight	120-proof Everclear, or substitute vodka
1 part	Sugar

1. Choose pears that are not too ripe. Combine ingredients in a blender.

2. Purée. Pass through a Chinois or the finest mesh sieve of a tamis.

3. Bottle and refrigerate if keeping for more than two days.

ROYAL SCANDINAVIAN CORDIAL

Yet another Jack of All Trades, working beautifully with everything from vodka and cognac to tequila and Calvados. When a small portion of this is mixed with vodka (about 1:5), it is an excellent version of the flavored vodka apertif presented gratis in many fine dining restaurants in Finland (served ice cold).

90ml (3 oz)	*Quality Lingonberry Juice
45ml (1½ oz)	White Wine, dry
30ml (1 oz)	Lemon Juice
2 teaspoons	Black Currant, dried powder
1 teaspoon	Lemon Zest
½ teaspoon	Licorice, dry powder
¼ teaspoon	Cardamom, seeds only (no pods)
¼ teaspoon	Sage, dried
140g (5 oz)	Sugar
50ml (1.75 oz)	Everclear 120 proof, or substitute vodka
15ml (½ oz)	Cognac, Hennessy *VS*
5 drops	Grapefruit Oil
3 drops	Lime Oil

1. In a saucepan or pot, combine all of the ingredients except the Everclear (or vodka), cognac, grapefruit oil and lime oil. Lingonberry juice is preferred, if possible.

2. On a medium-low heat, bring to a slow simmer with stirring.

3. Maintain at a slow simmer for 5 minutes.

4. Take off the heat and let steep for another 5 minutes.

5. Pass the solution through a Chinois twice. Discard the solids.

6. Add the Everclear (or vodka) and the cognac. Stir.

7. Transfer to a bottle using a funnel. Add the grapefruit and lime oils to the bottle. Swirl to combine. No refrigeration is needed unless you are going to keep this a long time. In that case, cold will preserve the freshness.

THE OTHER ORANGE LIQUEUR

Orange liqueurs are an essential ingredient in vast number of cocktails. There are only three common choices, Grand Marnier, Cointreau and Triple Sec. The latter of which is an inferior version of Cointreau invented for bars so they could save money. If you care about quality there are only two choices for orange liqueurs. Here is a third one, different from either of the classic two, but it can be swapped for Cointreau or Grand Marnier in many cocktails.

100ml (3.5 oz)	Orange Juice
30ml (1 oz)	Lemon Juice
25g (0.9 oz)	Orange Peel cut into strips, no pith
½ teaspoon	Fennel Seeds
½ teaspoon	Cloves, whole
¼ teaspoon	Coriander Seeds
2 whole	Roses, dried – crumbled (culinary grade)
150g (5.3 oz)	Sugar
1 teaspoon	Maraschino Liqueur, Luxardo
⅛ teaspoon	Orange Food color, powdered
90ml (3 oz)	Cognac, Hennessy *VS*
30ml (1 oz)	Everclear 120 proof
1 teaspoon	Maraschino Liqueur, Luxardo
5 drops	Orange Oil

1. In a small pot or saucepan, combine all of the ingredients except the cognac, Everclear, maraschino liqueur and orange oil.

2. On a medium-low heat, bring to a simmer while stirring often.

3. Reduce the heat and maintain at a simmer for 10 minutes, stirring.

4. Remove from the heat and let steep for 5-10 minutes more.

5. Pass through the finest mesh of a tamis. Discard the solids.

6. Add the cognac and the maraschino liqueur. Stir.

7. Transfer to a bottle using a funnel. Add the orange oil and swirl to combine. Keep refrigerated to retain freshness.

THE OTHER GRENADINE SYRUP

One of the most common cocktail ingredients is grenadine. Most of the common commercial brands have very little taste other than sugar syrup. There are some artisinal brands that are rich in pomegranate flavor, and those are just fine. Here is one that adds complexity and depth as well as pomegranate flavor and some sweetness. Be aware that this is roughly half as sweet as most commercial grenadines, so if you are using this in a recipe outside of this book, you will need to increase the amount.

Dark corn syrup does not contain high fructose corn syrup, and it does contain some molasses. This is especially useful in much of Europe where molasses is otherwise unavailable.

350ml (12.3 oz)	Pomegranate Juice, bottled; unsweetened
120g (4.2 oz)	Dark Corn Syrup
2 teaspoons	Lime Zest, grated
½ teaspoon	Orange Zest, grated
1 teaspoon	White Peppercorns, whole
½ teaspoon	Coriander Seeds

1. In a pot on the stove, combine all of the ingredients.

2, Heat to bring to a slow boil. That is, more than a simmer but not a full rolling boil. Stir frequently to make sure it does not boil over. Maintain at a slow boil for about 15 minutes.

3. Pass through the finest mesh of a tamis. If you have cooked this the correct amount, the volume should now be about 200ml (7 oz).

4. Transfer to a bottle using a funnel. This does not need refrigeration unless you are going to keep it for a long time.

✦

FERMENTED SALTY KUMQUAT LIQUEUR

This is a really unusual one. You can scale this up as much as you want to. This pairs especially well with tequila and mezcal.

120g (4.2 oz)	Kumquats, fresh
50ml (1.75 oz)	Vodka
50g (1.75 oz)	Dark Corn Syrup
½ teaspoon	Salt, ordinary table salt

1. Slice each kumquat in half.

2. Put the halves into a bowl and add the salt. Mix them around.

3. Seal under vacuum in a plastic bag.

4. Put a date on the bag and store away for 5-10 days until the bag is swollen up like a balloon as shown in the photo below.

5. Cut the bag open and empty the contents into a food processer. You can smell a beautiful alcohol aroma, and nothing rotten at all! Add the dark corn syrup and vodka. Purée for about 30 seconds.

6. Pass the mixture through the finest mesh of a tamis. Discard the solids.

7. Transfer to a jar to store. Refrigeration is needed for prolonged storage.

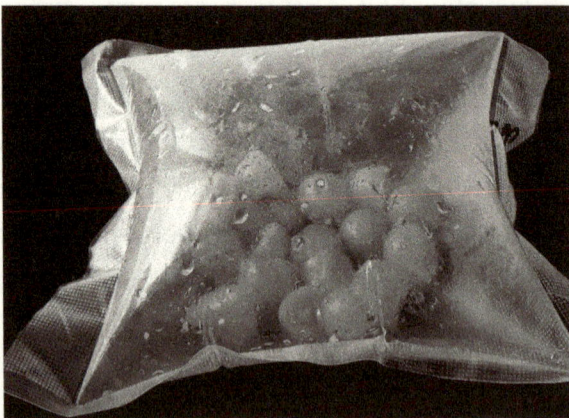

HOMEMADE COCONUT RUM

So you've had enough of Malibu and want to up your game? It is actually quite easy, and once you try this, you'll never go back.

300ml (10.6 oz)	Light Rum, Plantation 3-Star
60g (2 oz)	Coconut, dried and unsweetened
60g (2 oz)	Sugar

1. Put all of the ingredients into the same kind of pressure canister used to make whipped cream. Close it up and charge with 2 nitrous cartridges. Do not use more than 2 cartridges for safety reasons.

2, Leave it at room temperature for 24 to 48 hours, giving it a shake from time to time.

3. Release the pressure and strain the contents through a Chinois or very fine mesh sieve. Unlike the commercial product, this needs to be refrigerated because there are no preservatives in it.

4. Refrigerate. It actually improves over the course of a few days.

+

HOMEMADE MACADAMIA NUT RUM

This same principle can be used with other syrups such as lychee, walnut, etc.

4 parts	Light Rum, Plantation 3-Star
2 parts	Macadamia Nut Syrup, Monin
1 part	Plantation OFTD Rum

1. Combine all ingredients in a glass bottle with a stopper.

2. Close the lid and shake to mix. No refrigeration is needed, but keep it out of direct sunlight.

ORANGE IV SYRUP

This is the only recipe that has been repeated from a previous book; In this case, Volume 4 of my cookbook series (which is why it has been named Orange IV Syrup here). It is simple to prepare and is a very useful syrup that is seldom seen in commercial bottlings of high quality.

1 Large	Orange, fresh
300g (10.5 oz)	Sugar, white granulated
6 drops	Orange Oil

1. Peel the outermost layer of the orange using a vegetable peeler. Try not to get too much pith, but a little is okay. Put this into a saucepan.

2. Juice the orange. Put the saucepan on a scale and then add the juice. Add enough water to bring up the total weight to 300 grams (10.5 oz).

3. Add 300 grams (10.5 oz) of sugar to the pan. Heat on a medium flame to bring to a slow simmer for 15 minutes.

4. Turn off the heat and allow it to steep for another 15 minutes before pouring it through a very fine mesh sieve.

5. Transfer to a bottle using a funnel. Add the orange oil.

AUTO-FERMENTATION

6. Refrigeration is not necessary, but if you keep it at room temperature for about 2 months, it will begin to ferment spontaneously. The resulting product is interesting in its own right, but different from what is expected in a typical recipe.

＋

QUALITY LINGONBERRY JUICE

The product sold in stores (if you can even find it) is mostly water, as you can see from the color.

500ml (17.6 oz)	Apple Juice
500g (17.6 oz)	Lingonberries, frozen

1. Combine ingredients in a sauce pan.

2. Bring to a boil while stirring. As soon as it reaches a full boil, turn off the heat.

3. Wait 5 minutes, then transfer to a blender. Work in batches if your blender is not large enough to do it all at once.

4. Pass through a sieve. Then pass through a Chinois or the finest mesh of a tamis two times. The second pass will remove any small fibers.

5. Bottle. Refrigerate if you are going to keep it more than 2 days.

RUSSIAN MILK LIQUEUR

Do not substituted canned evaporated milk. That's entirely different. The international brand that works best is Nestle's for this. If you are in Russia, then there are brands that are even better, but you probably already know about that, then.

2 parts	Sweetened Condensed Milk, canned
1 part	Vodka

1. Combine ingredients in a jar with a lid. Put the lid on and shake vigorously to dissolve.

2. Store in the refrigerator. If you have not used this for a while, make sure it has not spoiled first.

LIGHT COCONUT SYRUP

One of the problems with the canned sweetened coconut called for in many cocktails is that it is too sweet and too concentrated. This will not overpower other ingredients and tastes natural.

150g (5.3 oz)	Coconut Milk, canned; unsweetened
50g (1.75 oz)	*Barley Base (page 171)
150g (5.3 oz)	Coconut Sugar, or substitute regular sugar
15ml (½ oz)	Macadamia Syrup, Monin (optional)
½ teaspoon	Vanilla Extract

1. In a pot on the stove, combine all of the ingredients.

2. Heat slowly to dissolve all of the sugar.

3. When it is completely dissoved, pass through a very fine mesh sieve and bottle. Store in the refrigerator because it is quite perishable.

IMITATION OF KYRO DAIRY CREAM

This is a liqueur unique to Finland, but critical in one of the best selling cocktails at Laava: The White Wedding. On more than one occasion, someone insisted they don't drink cocktails but after a few sips from a friend's they proceeded to order and drink several of these. Although it is better with the original Kyro liqueur, it's still a very good dessert cocktail. Try using this in place of Bailey's.

90g (3 oz)	Cream
45g (1½ oz)	Milk
22.5ml (¾ oz)	Rye Whiskey, Jim Beam
22.5ml (¾ oz)	Dark Corn Syrup
1 teaspoon	Fireball Liqueur

1. Combine all ingredients in a bottle and shake to combine.

2. Store refrigerated for up to a week, or until it sours.

HOMEMADE APRICOT COGNAC

This is an excellent and very quickly made apricot brandy useful in most recipes, and better than the cheap brands.

2 parts	Cognac, Hennessy V.S.
1 part	Apricot Preserves, ideally St. Dalfour

1. Combine ingredients in a jar and shake vigorously to dissolve as much of the jam into the cognac as possible. If you have time, leave it to stand for a while, shaking occassionally. This will improve it.

2. Strain through a sieve. No refrigeration is required.

✦

DARK APRICOT BRANDY

This will produce an unusual product, and as a bonus you get brandy-macerated apricots to use as a garnish (see Planet of the Apricots recipe on page 159).

per 60g (2 oz)	Dried Apricots, non-sulphured
1 Tablespoon	Sugar
to cover	Spanish Brandy, Torres 10

1. Use a jar that is tall and narrow. Put the apricots in with the sugar (1 tablespoon for each 60 grams (2 ounces) of dried apricots.

2. Add enough brandy to cover the apricots.

3. Let stand for 2 to 3 days (no more than 3!) with occasional shaking. As the apricots absorb the brandy, top it off with more brandy. It's important to be patient and wait at least two days before continuing.

4. Strain the contents through a sieve. Keep the macerated apricots for use as a garnish, or to chop up and put in a fruit cake if you bake. No refrigeration is needed for the brandy. The apricots should be kept cold.

LAVENDER SUGAR

The inherent problem with using lavender or rose flavors is they tend to remind people of bath soaps in a most unpleasant way, so care must be taken to avoid overuse. This is intended as a sugar for rimming the glass of a cocktail containing Crème de Violette or Parfait Amour. It is slightly subtle, but very effective.

8 parts	Sugar, white granulated
1 part	Lavender, culinary grade

1. Put the mixture into a food processor. Grind for 15-20 seconds.

2. Pass the mixture through a metal sieve. Discard the solid lavender that would not pass through. This does not need refrigeration, however the aroma and flavor fade quite rapidly. It should be used right away.

⁘

LAAVA UNICORN MATRIX ZERO

The concept of a Matrix is fully explained in my previous book, *Cocktails of the South Pacific*. A Matrix formula was used in a many recipes at Laava, but most of those formulas relied on local Finnish ingredients that are not obtainable elsewhere.

25%	Cointreau
20%	Vana Tallinn, ideally 45% ABV
15%	Crème de Noyeaux, Tempis Fugit
10%	Maraschino Liqueur, Maraska
10%	Dubonnet
7.5%	Raspberry Syrup, Monin
7.5%	Ginger Liqueur, Bols
5%	Apricot Liqueur, Merlet
2 drops per 100ml	Orange Oil (see text below)

1. Combine all ingredients in a jar or bottle. Add 2 drops of orange oil for every 100ml (3.5 oz) of the mixture. No refrigeration is needed.

BERGAMOT BITTERS

There are several commercial brands of bergamot bitters on the market, but I prefer this homemade variety. The downside is that it takes a very long time to become ready for use.

1 part	Bergamot Peel (see below)
4 parts	Vodka

1. Use a vegetable peeler on a bergamot orange to peel it. Get mostly the zest with only a little of the pith in each slice. Juice the fruit, too.

2. Place the peelings in a narrow jar and add the vodka with a *little* of the juice (about 10% by volume). Close the lid and store away from light. Shake it up about once a day for about 2 weeks.

3. Remove the peel and carefully decant the clear liquid. Transfer to a fresh clean bottle with a loose screw lid (for slow evaporation). At this point you have **Bergamot Zest Extract** (see recipe below).

4. Store another 2-3 months before decanting again. No refrigeration needed.

✦

EARLY BIRD COCKTAIL

"The early bird gets the worm, but the early worm gets eaten."

Here is a brunch cocktail that will let you sample your bergamot bitters early. This showcases how bergamot is like a rich pefrume.

75ml (2½ oz)	White Rum, Plantation 3-Star
15ml (½ oz)	Lime Juice, strained
15ml (½ oz)	Grenadine (the commercial product this time)
1 teaspoon	*Fassionola
1 teaspoon	*Bergamot Zest Extract (see recipe above)
1 dash	Grapefruit Bitters, Fee Bros.

Combine all ingredients. Shake with ice and then either serve straight up or on cracked ice with a straw, as desired.

CONCLUSION

This book will not do you any good left laying dormant on a shelf collecting dust. Nor will it do you very much good if you just pick out a few recipes to try, regardless of whether you love those drinks, or even if you don't happen to care for them personally (after all, there is no way to present dozens of recipes that everyone will love).

In the end, a few of the recipes here are for fun, and those are pretty obvious. Some have been included because they were received so well by so many customers that there is a good chance they will become your favorites, too...

BUT...

...most of the recipes here are to illustrate the system explained between pages 59 and 68, even if that isn't obvious at first glance. In fact, if you only read *those ten pages*, this book will very likely have changed your outlook on mixology forever, even if you're already a seasoned professional.

With all of the years that went into the research, the long nights, the thousands of experiments, and the liquor for those experiments that the sales of this book couldn't begin to pay back the cost of, now it is left up to you to have made it all worthwhile. Cheers!

INDEX

ITEMS IN ITALICS = COCKTAIL RECIPE

A

H

I

J

K

T

NOTES

NOTES

www.ingramcontent.com/pod-product-compliance
Lightning Source LLC
Chambersburg PA
CBHW031250090426
42742CB00007B/385